D1636248

Adlerian Family Counseling

(Revised Edition)

A Manual for Counselor, Educator, and Psychotherapist

Edited by

Oscar C. Christensen

University of Arizona
Tucson, Arizona

94-102

Library of Congress Catalog Card No. 93-70537
ISBN 0-932796-56-7
Printing (Last Digit)
9 8 7 6 5 4 3 2 1

Production editor—

Don L. Sorenson, Ph.D.

Graphic Design—

Earl Sorenson

Table of Contents

Contributors

Oscar C. Christensen, Professor, Counseling and Guidance Program, University of Arizona, Tucson, Arizona

William C . Marchant, Psychologist, Las Vegas, Nevada

Carroll R. Thomas, Psychologist, Las Vegas, Nevada

Lynn O'Hern-Hall, Counselor, Tucson, Arizona

Frank Williams, Assistant Director, 4-H Youth Development, Cooperative Extension, University of Arizona, Tucson, Arizona

Gary D. McKay, Writer, consultant, licensed psychologist, Communication and Motivation Training Institute—West, Tucson, Arizona

Joyce McKay, Writer, consultant, certified professional counselor, Communication and Motivation Training Institute—West, Tucson, Arizona

E Clair Hawes, Psychologist, North Vancouver, British Columbia

Raymond Lowe, Professor, Department of Counseling Psychology, University of Oregon, Eugene, Oregon

Oscar C. Christensen, Ed.D.

Overview

This book provides the reader with an introduction to the principles and practices of Adlerian family counseling. The structure of the American, Canadian, and other families has undergone a dramatic change in the past 40 years. The increase in single-parent families, stepfamilies, and foster families is a matter of record. As a result of these changes, family counselors and therapists are forced to emphasize education and presentation, as well as family counseling.

The principles of Adlerian family counseling described here provide an in-depth understanding of patterns of family development and growth. These principles give the reader a practical framework to apply to Adlerian family counseling.

The initial chapter by Christensen and Marchant provides a systematic orientation to family counseling—an orientation which is a theme for succeeding chapters. Following chapters detail assessment techniques, counselor-child interaction, and psychodramatic techniques according to the Christensen and Marchant framework. Applications to the training of family counselor and marriage counseling include similar systematic guides in their structure.

Each of these chapters helps the reader to understand the elements involved in the education and training of family counselors, as well as the practice of Adlerian family counseling. Models and flow charts are added to assist the readers in assessing their work as family counselors, without suggesting that such models are an inflexible mold for family or marriage counseling. To the contrary, readers are encouraged to reconceptualize the process in any manner that facilitates their practice of Adlerian family counseling.

Introduction

The structure of the American family has undergone unbelievable, though understandable, changes in the last 35 years. The increase in single parent families, reconstituted families, blended families, stepfamilies, and foster families is a matter of record. These structural changes, however, have had little effect on the purpose and basic interpersonal relationships of the family group. Regardless of these "new" groupings, the family is still the social unit which is charged with the rearing, socialization, and education of the young. As a result, family counselors and therapists are forced to shift their emphasis to include education and prevention as part of their repertoire of skills.

The purpose of the book is to provide the reader a collection of principles and practices employed by experienced family counselors who have been influenced by the teaching of Rudolf Dreikurs and subscribe to the psychological theory of Alfred Adler. It was Dreikurs who clarified and refined Adler's original work on family counseling making Adlerian family counseling a viable force in counselor education throughout the United States and Canada. Dreikurs and his students have brought about a change in the traditional counseling approach deemphasizing a cause and effect model in favor of one which emphasizes change through an understanding of the intent of individual behavior. General strategies and specific techniques that can facilitate change are explicated in this book. Throughout the book there is a continual emphasis on learning and teaching through case exemplification.

Oscar C. Christensen, Ed.D.

Chapter 1

The Rationale
for
Family Counseling

by Oscar C. Christensen

The structure of the American family has undergone unbelievable, even though understandable, changes in the last 35 years. The
increase in one-parent families, reconstituted families, blended families, stepfamilies, and foster families is a matter of record. These
structural changes, however, have had relatively little effect on the
purpose or basic interpersonal relationships of the family group.
Regardless of the "new" groupings, the family is still the social unit
which is charged with the rearing, socialization, and education of
the young. Regardless of the cosmetic changes which are observable
to the most casual observer, the really significant change has taken
place in the interaction patterns of the adults and their children,
regardless of composition of the various groups called the family.

One of the problems created by social observers who operate on
a reductionistic cause-and-effect concept of science is that "effects"
are frequently attributed to the most available "cause." The "break-
down" of the family and "eroding family values" are all too often
attributed to the observed changes in composition, size, and mobil-
ity. While assigning a cause generally serves the purpose of scholar-
ship, it rarely offers real understanding or possibilities for solutions.

To understand the problems faced by today's parents adequately, one must become aware of the changes that have taken place which affect the traditional systems for child-rearing and adult-child relationships. The relationship between parent and child has undergone profound and basic modifications and rarely is the parent or child aware of the new order. Each, therefore, lives in conflict and tension, each side self-righteously blaming the other for the problem.

Having a traditional model or system for child rearing is not unique to the American culture. Every society in the world has its cultural traditions for parenting and adult-child relationships. Regardless of variations, all traditions have in common the unspoken hope that the methods employed will produce the type of adult who can best survive in that culture. The other generalization is that the elevation of a child-rearing practice to the status of a tradition is a lengthy process, so that by the time a particular practice is institutionalized as a tradition, it may be a century or two out-of-date. If one views child-rearing as initial societal survival training, then the compatibility of the child training and the reality of contemporary society is essential. To more fully understand the bankruptcy of traditional American parenting, it might be useful to outline the origin of American child-rearing traditions.

It is interesting that nearly all child-rearing practices termed "traditional" and employed on this continent are, in fact, European. One of the unfortunate realities of the melting pot of America is that we "melted out" our Asian and African traditions and have reduced our Native American heritage to a vague memory. The result is that the dominant culture pattern for child-rearing still held as "American" is, in most respects, European. However, it is the Europe of the pre-immigration era of our history. In fact, we still model many, if not most, of our interpersonal relationships upon the traditions of 19th century Europe. Basically, the European model was an autocratic social system where all interpersonal relationships were based upon superior-inferior relationships. The king was considered better than the nobles, the nobles better than the peasants. Even within the lowest of the serfs' huts, the males were superior to the females and the adults of greater value than the children.

This social order necessitated child training that would insure that children would survive the social system they were growing up to inherit. It was an absolute necessity that children learn to bow and scrape, since as adults they would be expected to do likewise. To be "seen and not heard" or "speak when spoken to," like most cliches of childhood, had their origins in our collective autocratic heritage. Obviously, the system worked, the child was trained to have an appropriate slave mentality suitable for survival as an inferior. Many of the "problems" often reported are, in fact, the climax of 500 years of democratic revolutions, culminating after World War II in the civil rights movement and women's liberation. In this same time span the last minority, children, also won their equality.

One of the alarming and obvious facts of life is that the only training for becoming a parent is to have been a child. This suggests that today's parents, for the most part, parent from the same model that their parents provided. Basically, the model provided was an autocratic model. There is nothing inherently wrong in the autocratic parenting model, except that it is inappropriate for today's child. The inappropriateness of the autocratic parent's attempting to rear a child aware of equality should be obvious. Unfortunately, neither parent nor child is aware of the discrepancy and therefore both are confused by the dialogue that ensues.

If one assumes the parent is speaking down to the child from the position of superior, while the child listens and reacts from a position of equality, the communication is lost.

Further, when children respond to their parents from their perceived position of equal, the parental shock and dismay are understandable. When a parent complains of a child who "sasses" or "talks back," that parent should tape record 45 minutes of interaction with their children. Inevitably, the tape recording will reveal that "back talk" reported is precisely the mode of speech employed by the parent to the child. In an authoritarian model, it is apparently all right for an adult to talk disrespectfully to children, but the converse is a high crime. The interaction pattern in family after family is of the parent talking "down" to children and children talking "disrespectfully equal" to parents.

The concern becomes magnified when one realizes that this represents the same interaction pattern between teacher and student in the classroom.

The lack of understanding by parents of the emerging equality of youth has led to further complications in the interactive process. Typically many parents either attempt to overpower the child to reassert the superiority of the adult over the child or to capitulate, to give up and give in to the child. The either-or, win-lose resolution has tragic results.

In those instances where the parent has attempted to reassert authority by forcing the child into an inferior position, two general outcomes have been observed. One is the intensification and escalation of the struggle, unwittingly forcing the child into more defiant and open rebellion. The second outcome is the apparent successful subjection of the child. In this case the child either accepts domination, with the projected problems of becoming a dominated or dominating adult, or demonstrates passivity in the parents' company while acting out in private or with peers. None of these outcomes of the parent-child struggle is desirable. All tend to violate the ideal of a parent-child relationship based upon mutual respect.

The concept of mutual respect is a necessary component for an egalitarian relationship, though very few people appear to understand the meaning of the term "equality." The vast majority of people in the United States, when asked to define equality, will respond "to be the same." Sameness is not an adequate definition of equality. In fact, sameness violates the concept of individual differences inherent in a democratic society. All too often, the vigorous opponents and proponents of women's liberation are debating sameness, not equality. Men and women are not the same. The French resolved this issue several centuries ago with the expression *viva la difference*. Children and adults are not the same, but they are equal.

The conceptualization of equality that allows obvious differences to occur is the concept of equality of value, of worth, or the equality of personhood. By accenting the concept of equality of value rather than sameness, it is possible to define different roles for parent and child without violating mutual respect. The parent is the leader and not the boss, the teacher, the child's counselor. The child may then become the learner without being expected to act or feel inferior. The respect that parents desire from their children can be taught by modeling the same respect for the children.

Another concept which is useful in understanding family dynamics is that of family atmosphere. The family atmosphere is created by the parents and is the means by which all social values as well as family values are transmitted to the offspring. The interpersonal relationship between mother and father becomes the model for the relationships between siblings. Caring or uncaring, loving or punishing, cooperative or competitive atmospheres are all taught by the relationship demonstrated by the parents in their interactions with each other.

Oscar C. Christensen, Ed.D.

One generalization that characterizes an extremely high percentage of American marriages is competition. The competitive marriage is the result of the unresolved issue of male and female equality. Most marriages today are still subtle battlegrounds for male supremacy while women either subjugate themselves or fight back. In either case, the model for sibling interaction is one of superior-inferior status.

Each child must compete for one's position in the family. It is this factor above all others that accounts for the wide differences in the apparent abilities, talents, and personalities that are observed between and among children in the same family. Competition forces the eldest to attempt to maintain the position of first and best, while the second child must either try harder and overtake the eldest or find other means of obtaining significance. Each ordinal position offers the child who occupies it a different vantage point for interpreting life and estimating how best to compete in finding one's place in the family. There are as many variations on the theme as there are children, but some similarities of personality as a result of birth order have been noted over the years by many psychologists.

The important factor, however, is not the usefulness of the predictability of personality associated with birth order, but an understanding of the competitive striving which creates the need to be different, to be unique, to excel at the expense of other siblings in the family. The competition associated with this phenomenon is destructive, since the competition forces many youngsters to seek significance on the negative side of life. The same driving ambition that pushes the scholar to higher marks may, in many more families, drive an eldest child to be the best at being worst, or the youngest child to compensate for feeling smallest and weakest by becoming incapable, thus putting others in one's service.

Understanding the dynamics of today's family is extremely useful for those who must deal with youth and their parents with problems. The same understanding must also be employed to bring about significant changes in families to preclude the probability of problems.

One possible beginning point would be a change in the basic marriage relationship. If one could imagine a truly equal partnership without the domination of one party by the other, a start for appropriate sibling relationships would have been achieved. Adult-child relationships based upon mutual respect employing democratic principles for problem solving is a second step. Replacing competition with cooperation as a basis for family living would logically follow, thus permitting all of the children in a given family to select areas of accomplishment based upon interest and desire rather than feeling forced to "give up" when a brother or sister appears to be more effective in a given endeavor.

To accomplish such a monumental task, as re-educating an entire generation of parents and children to employ more appropriate relationship models, is indeed awesome. However, many communities have made modest and successful beginnings. The Parent Study Group movement developed by followers of Rudolf Dreikurs, utilizing the text *Children: The Challenge* (Dreikurs & Soltz, 1964), or the *STEP* program devised by Dinkmeyer and McKay (1976), has proven to be an effective means of providing the necessary information and education for change (see Parent Study Groups, Chapter 7).

Concerted efforts by professionals to shift the emphasis of counseling delivery systems from remediation to prevention are evidence that many counselors are aware of the growing need to change, and thereby preserve, the family as an institution. However, the changes that are required are those which will allow the family once again to provide children with survival skills, not the skills of an autocratic past but, rather, the skills of a democratic future.

References

Dreikurs, R., & Soltz, V. (1964). *Children: The challenge.* New York: Duell, Sloan, & Pearce.

Dinkmeyer, D., &. McKay, D. (1976). *Systematic training for effective parenting.* Circle Pines, MN: American Guidance Service.

Oscar C. Christensen, Ed.D.

Chapter 2

Basic Principles of Adlerian Family Counseling

by Carroll R. Thomas and William C. Marchant

Basic Assumptions About Human Nature

The practice of Adlerian family counseling is based upon principles of behavior articulated by Alfred Adler. The primary purpose of this chapter is to provide a brief summary of Adler's basic assumption about human nature. The second purpose is to relate these assumptions to the practice of Adlerian family counseling.

These principles are also outlined in *The Individual Psychology of Alfred Adler,* edited by Heinz and Rowen Ansbacher (1956), and more recently in the book, *Individual Psychology: Theory and Practice,* by Manaster and Corsini (1982).

Holism and Uniqueness

Adler chose to call his psychology "Individual Psychology," consistent with the Latin word *individuum,* meaning the indivisible individual. Thus, Adler's psychology is a holistic psychology, emphasizing that each individual is best understood as a totality. In contrast, many psychological theories attempt to reduce the individual to the smallest unit of behavior in order to achieve understanding. Adlerians believe that the individual is *more than* the sum of the behaviors. The human is viewed as the integration of interacting systems of behavior.

A good example of this assumption is human speech. In the human body there is no single organ which is solely designed for speech. Each of the organs used for speech seems to be designed as a component of some other system or function, such as breathing or masticating. If we attempt to isolate human speech in single system parts, we end up unable to understand the process of speech. Human speech is best viewed as a function of the interactions of several different, but overlapping, systems in the body.

So it is with the personality. When we attempt to understand the personality atomistically, rather than holistically, we lose the ability to understand the individual human being as a unique and interactive totality.

Phenomenology

Adler's psychology is a phenomenological psychology. That is, we believe that the facts of one's life are not as important as one's perception of those facts. It is assumed that each individual perceives the world in a unique fashion. Consequently, Adlerian psychology has been correctly called a psychology of use rather than a psychology of possession. This view is consistent with most theories which emphasize individual responsibility for one's actions, because those actions have, to a large degree, been created by the way in which one interprets events. Kelly (1955) suggested the same principle when he formulated his fundamental postulate that human processes are "psychologically channelized" by the way in which one interprets events.

Social Embeddedness

Adlerians view people as existing within a social framework. Consequently, the individual is seen as socially embedded in interacting social systems. Adlerian counselors assume that one can be most successful in helping an individual to change if one can change the way one system (family) interprets and responds to the individual's behavior. Hence, the primary unit of intervention is the family.

Purposive Behavior

A logical extension of the foregoing is the notion that behavior is purposive. Adler conceptualized that all behavior was characterized by movement toward a goal. Typically, individuals move away from feelings of inferiority toward feelings of growth, completeness, and wholeness. The individual strives to overcome perceived difficulties. Such behavior is described as goal-directed, future-oriented, teleological, or purposive. Purposive behavior is an important assumption, as it guides the Adlerian family counselor in developing strategies for behavioral and attitudinal change.

Social Equality

Equality is a term which is often misunderstood. The term "social equality," as used here, refers to equality in terms of worth and value. We assume that people are of equal value, but not the same. We assume the likelihood of everyone having the competencies necessary to make some kind of a contribution. Consistent with the notion of purposive behavior, we have an expectation that everyone can make a contribution for the benefit of a social system, whether it be a dyadic relationship, a family, or a community.

Adlerians believe in the golden rule of reciprocity: Do unto others as you would have others do unto you. This implies that we do have responsibilities for each other. It suggests that there is a higher order of social living than merely "looking out for number one." The inescapable conclusion from the foregoing is that children as well as adults have human rights as well as responsibilities.

Mutual Respect

The primary goal of the family is to establish relationships which increase the group's feeling of well-being. The children's initial responsibility is to contribute to a reasonable family routine. A parental responsibility is to establish a sensible waking-sleeping schedule and encourage the children to develop a pattern consistent with it. The child's next responsibility is to contribute to the family welfare. The parent's next responsibility is to provide the necessary guidance and structure in which this can take place. Children are expected not to demand unnecessary services or assistance, especially in activities they can perform for themselves. If parents submit to undue demands, they allow themselves to become victimized and exploited by the children. Such children quickly become tyrants. All members of the family have responsibilities and should be expected to perform them routinely.

In a well-functioning family, all members work to the best of their ability so that all family members may enjoy maximum pleasure, comfort, satisfaction, and happiness, and a minimum of pain, discomfort, dissatisfaction, and unhappiness. Everyone fully respects everyone else and does not allow anyone to be treated disrespectfully. The family becomes a mutually cooperative team. The formula for the success of such a family is *mutual respect*—respect for one's self; respect for others.

It is best to relate with children—as well as with one another—according to kind firmness: the logic contained in the Golden Rule. If we treat others with disrespect, we can also expect to be treated with disrespect. Each person has the right to be respected, which, in this context, means that no unreasonable requests or demands be made of anyone. Children should not be considered pets, playthings, toys, or idiots. Unfortunately, this is precisely how many adults view children—as lovable, cute incompetent things to play with or criticize.

Making children into royalty is also disrespectful. A child may be a little prince or princess at home, but will not have this glorified status on the playground, at school, or later in life. Respect is characterized by honest, truthful evaluation and treatment. Stimulating children to become dependent by providing too many unnecessary services, by not allowing them to make decisions, or by over-protection is disrespectful and does them a great deal of harm.

Adults can help children in their development toward socially constructive orientation by utilizing a logical, rational, and egalitarian approach. Some behaviors are considered "appropriate" or "valid." Other behaviors are considered "inappropriate" or "invalid." "Good" behavior is encouraged, supported, and reinforced while "bad" behavior is not encouraged, supported, or reinforced. Appropriateness is viewed as a function of self and other-respect. Thus, in any situation, the crucial questions are always: "Does the adult show respect for the child? Does the child show respect for the adult? Does each individual show respect for one's self?"

Love and Affection

Love, tenderness, mutuality, affection, and good will are advocated by Adlerians, but they are considered *consequences* or *effects* of respectful relationships, rather than causes of such relationships. Parents can genuinely love their newborn baby before exposure to the child, but to maintain positive feelings for the child, the child has to earn and deserve them. It seems that we can unconditionally love, respect, and accept a person's *being*, while we conditionally love, respect, and accept a person's *doing*. We can separate the deed from the doer.

Children who make genuine efforts are respectful, cooperate, contribute, and otherwise show that they mean well. Parents who behave in a similar manner are also loved by their children. Love is an emotion, and emotions are the result of beliefs, thoughts, opinions, and evaluations, not their cause. More important than emotions are intellect, reason, and action. We can train our minds to understand, and we can train our bodies to function appropriately; but, we cannot as readily train our emotions. The crucial mistake made by many parents is that they equate love with their own desires and think eagerness to serve, obey, and comply with their children's demands represents love. Both the submissive, slave-like approach and the autocratic, aggressive, tyrant-like approach are equally harmful.

Cultural Changes

The cultural changes we are experiencing are the birth pains of an almost totally new epoch of human relationships. Three major phases in the social evolution of humanity can be distinguished: a primitive society, an autocratic society, and the present emerging democratic society. A democratic society does not simply imply political and economic changes—it suggests basic changes in *all* human relationships. In the autocratic society, one was either in a superior and dominant position or in an inferior and subordinate position. In a democratic society, each individual is equal in terms of personal worth, value, and dignity as well as rights and responsibilities.

In all cultures and civilizations throughout history, child-rearing has followed a traditional pattern. One reason for our present predicament in raising children is the lack of an established tradition. The present generation is faced with a changing social atmosphere in which the traditional methods of raising children are becoming obsolete. As a result of this change, parents are often confused and bewildered about what to do with their children. Moreover, the professional and expert advice they frequently receive only adds to their confusion.

We are living in a different social atmosphere from that of our parents and grandparents. Reward and punishment as methods of control have lost their effectiveness in a democratic society which does not support such approaches. Both reward and punishment were consistent with an autocratic culture as a means by which people in power could enforce their will upon their subordinates. Society, in turn, supported the rights of parents to employ every imaginable means of compelling submission and compliance, even severe beatings. Today's society, however, sides with children and declares a brutal and cruel parent unfit. Today, children draw only one conclusion when punished: "If you have the right to punish me, then I have the right to punish you." Children view rewards as their rights and think parents are ridiculous to try to discipline or control them by such measures (see Rationale for Family Counseling, Chapter 1).

Discipline

Adults, by nature of their larger size and wider repertoire of knowledge, skills, and experience, have historically disciplined their children by *forcing* them into compliance. Traditionally, the conflict between the generations was contained by the power and authority of adults. Juvenile delinquency and childhood schizophrenia express the extreme forms of rebellion of today's youth. Children feel mistreated and misunderstood, and adults feel disrespected and defeated. When people do want to change this situation, they often erroneously assume that they can become democratic simply by refraining from being autocratic. However, merely refraining from being autocratic often leads to permissiveness and over-indulgence.

Only recently have better methods been developed. The new approach assumes that every person strives toward a distinct goal with a dedication and singleness of purpose. Thus, in order to understand and guide children, we begin by identifying and understanding the goals toward which they strive. We discover which goals are constructive and adaptive and which are destructive and maladaptive. Then, we apply specific methods to correct the situation. Adults need to understand what they can and cannot do with children in times of conflict. Since external force is no longer effective, they have to learn approaches which encourage an inner motivation toward cooperation, effective functioning, respect for social order, and fulfillment of the requirements of social living.

One such specific technique is the use of *natural* and *logical consequences* as methods of discipline (Dreikurs & Soltz, 1964). The constant use of rewards and punishments can be avoided if adults act so that children who misbehave experience the natural or logical consequences of their misbehavior. These consequences should be discussed before their application so the children know what to expect when they decide to misbehave—when they decide to violate the rules of social order. The rule of thumb in a democratic social order is *cooperate and contribute or experience the consequences of your decision*. Each family can function more smoothly and efficiently if it establishes its own norms and then lets its members experience the consequences of their behavior.

Natural and logical consequences express the essence of the logic of respectful interpersonal relationships. A mutual decision is made among different members of the family, and if anyone violates the terms of the agreement, that person experiences the consequences of the violation. Practically every aspect of life represents

Oscar C. Christensen, Ed.D.

some type of social contract. The state provides certain things to its citizens and expects certain things in return. If we misbehave by breaking the law, we may experience the consequences of our behavior either by paying a fine or by being imprisoned. If we violate the contract of our employment, we may soon be looking for another job. If we act with our friends in a way contrary to the unwritten social expectation of appropriate social-behavior, we may soon be looking for new friends. Only absolute tyrants with unlimited power and authority can do what they wish, when they wish, to whom they wish.

Conflict Resolution

Our tradition has not prepared us to live with one another as social equals. We often do not know how to resolve differences on the basis of mutual respect and social equality. In any conflict situation, we generally see a choice between fighting, with the chance of winning, or yielding, with the certainly of losing. As long as there are differences in interests, intentions, and goals, there will be conflicts. It follows that the most crucial consideration is how we resolve these conflicts. Differences and disagreements can no longer be settled by force as they once were. The winner can no longer relax on the strength of victory because the loser is not willing to accept the winner's superiority and submit to it. As a result, most solutions achieved by traditional forms of conflict resolution are unsatisfactory and the struggle continues indefinitely.

The democratic approach does not avoid conflicts, but attempts to solve them. In an autocratic society, the person(s) with the most power made the decisions, and the others had to accept them. But in a democratic society, this is impossible because no one accepts the other's superiority. Fortunately, we can learn to solve conflicts, not avoid or fight over them, by seeking new mutual agreements. A mutual agreement is reached when everyone has gained something from the decision. Effective democratic conflict resolution includes the following basic ingredients: (1) mutual respect; (2) identifying and focusing on the real issue; (3) reaching a mutually acceptable agreement; and (4) mutual decision-making and responsibility-sharing (Dreikurs, Corsini, & Gould, 1975).

Family Constellation

In the process of family counseling, Adlerians rely on two important factors, incorporating the previous assumptions. *Family constellation* information gives the counselor important insights into what each family member may be bringing to the family interactions. Assessing *family atmosphere* will also help the counselor structure recommendations specifically to each situation.

Experiences in our family of origin—our opportunities, obstacles, problems, goals, frustrations, achievements—are all significantly influenced by our birth order position. Understanding these influences can assist us in formulating a more effective and efficient course in life and in helping others to do likewise.

Influence on Personality Development

Early experiences are some of the most important factors in the development of our personality or life style, which is our frame of reference for perceiving, and evaluating our world. The family is our first social reality, a reality from which we interpret, perceive, conclude, and generalize to the rest of the world. Thus, the knowledge, skills, and attitudes, acquired in our family of origin greatly influence our capacity for functioning in situations outside the family.

Behavior is viewed as an expression of the individual's creative movement, originating within the family unit. This is in contrast to other viewpoints which attribute personality development strictly to hereditary or environmental factors. The concept of family constellation directs the family counselor's attention to the individual's interpretations and resulting interactions with the world. We each influence other members of our family as we are influenced by them. Our own interpretations and resulting actions often stimulate others to treat us as we expect to be treated.

Each of us as children in a family also create, through trial and error, our own unique approaches in an effort to establish a place in the group. All our strivings are directed toward feelings of belonging and security. Consequently, we each train ourselves to develop attributes by which we hope to achieve significance and uniqueness within the family.

Individual Interpretation

Individuals often interpret and react differently to the same situation. Similarly, two children born into the same family actually live in exactly the same situation. The family environment surrounding each child may actually by quite different, with many significant changes occurring over time. For example, changes frequently occur in the family with the birth of each child, as parents become older and more experienced, as the family's social or economic status changes, as the family moves to another neighborhood or another area, or as parents divorce or die and the child gains a step-parent. Other factors frequently affecting the child's place within the family are: (1) an exceptional, sickly, or handicapped child; (2) a child born just before or after the death of another child; (3) an only boy among girls or an only girl among boys; (4) obvious physical characteristics such as being very attractive or very unattractive; (5) an elderly person such as a grandparent living in the home; and (6) parental favoritism.

According to Adler, the life style of every child is an imprint of a unique position within the family. He pointed out that much of our future attitude toward ourselves, others, and life depends precisely upon this one fact. Adler also stressed that it is not the birth order position per se which influences personality development, but rather the *psychological position,* the manner in which children interpret and respond to their position. Thus, birth order position provides a context in which an individual's life style will develop. With these thoughts in mind, the following generalizations are offered regarding birth order positions.

Birth Order

Most of us make assumptions about children's behavior. For example, the notion that two children from the same family should be alike seems to be based on the assumption that since they came from the same gene pool, they should be identical in behavior. This assumption can be questioned by examining one's family of origin and trying to remember if anyone in the family is identical. It's very doubtful that one will be able to demonstrate the sameness of individuals from the same family.

One can easily challenge the assumption that children should be alike even if their parents attempt to treat them alike. From the Adlerian view, no two children are ever born into the same family. Each child after the first is born into a different family system. The first child is born into a family that, until the time of birth, consisted of two people. The second child is born into a family that, until the time of birth, consisted of three people, and so on. Each child is entering a different social system. Until the birth of each succeeding child, the interrelationships within the family system have been uniquely defined. The arrival of the new child requires new definition of the family system. Within this context, it is difficult for any parent to raise succeeding children in an identical fashion. One can look, for example, at the very large family where the younger children are essentially raised by the older children.

The eldest child is for a limited time the only child. The eldest child is, therefore, quite likely to be the center of attention, to be a special object of care. In most families, a new brother or sister is thrust upon the child. The new child now monopolizes the parents. Consequently, the oldest child must redefine some personal hypotheses developed about the world. This child is no longer the cute one that everyone gathered around on a Sunday afternoon to watch do tricks. The eldest child now seems to attempt tricks at the wrong time—for example, just as mother is going to get the baby. It is not too far-fetched to recognize that the eldest child may develop a fear of being set aside in favor of the newcomer. This is very likely the genesis of the feeling of jealousy in the eldest.

Parents who have been very patient with the eldest until the birth of the new one very suddenly become impatient. The parents typically try to defend the second child against the oldest. The eldest's curiosity may be greeted by a shriek from mother, "Don't touch the baby!"

After a few of these experiences in living with a new member of the family, the oldest child typically develops some different hypotheses about how to maintain a positive position in the family. Eldest very frequently become cautious, examining all risks carefully before attempting new tasks. They may become somewhat shy and withdrawn, or attempt to show the parents that they are still "the good one" by making sure that the parent knows what the second child has done wrong.

It can become very important to the first child to maintain a superior position within the family for fear of being overtaken and surpassed by the next child. This fear of being overtaken and surpassed frequently results in oldest children putting severe demands on themselves for achievement, high standards of behavior, and even success at all costs. With such an overdeveloped ambition, eldest children will very often set standards for themselves that are seemingly unattainable, and, therefore, put themselves in a position of discouragement.

The second child, on the other hand, comes with a built-in pacemaker in the form of the eldest child. The second child never seems to lose sight of the one who has the short head start. And it's not very long before the second child realizes that the eldest is trying to maintain a superior position. Second children very frequently view everything that the oldest child can do as an indication of their own smallness and inferiority. Consequently, they try to catch up. The second child will typically attempt to achieve a superior position in areas where the oldest encounters difficulties.

With the birth of a third child, the second child now becomes the fabled middle child. Middle children tend to see themselves as having neither the same rights as the older nor the privileges of the younger. They consequently feel very squeezed. These are often the children who see a good deal of unfairness in life and feel cheated and abused. A typical phrase that is more common among middle children than others is "That's not fair."

In a very positive sense, however, middle children tend to be rather good survivors. From the point of view of a middle child, "As long as I've had to go through so much crap to get where I am, I might just as well continue on." And while they might adopt a rather cynical attitude toward life, they tend to survive quite well.

The youngest child comes into the world occupied by a good many older people. All of the other children are ahead in age, size, and competence. The little one is in a position to be spoiled by everyone. It is, therefore, not difficult to imagine that the youngest children would develop characteristics which make it likely that other people will help them shape their lives. Such characteristics as helplessness, a winning nature, and a whimsical smile are all manipulative devices which can be used by a youngest child.

More and more families are deciding to produce only one child. The only child, therefore, will likely become a more common occurrence. Only children tend to be personal comfort-oriented: that is, they have a feeling that they have a right to be comfortable in any situation. This kind of orientation results in the only child possessing many of the characteristics of the oldest child and, at the same time, many of the characteristics of the youngest child. Only children are likely to be relatively demanding, somewhat self-centered, somewhat controlling and very subtly manipulative in their approach to other people. In adulthood, the only child tends to have ambivalent feelings about childhood. This ambivalence is relatively easy to understand when one realizes that only children have always existed in an adult world. When they finally get to be adults, they become somewhat more comfortable with their situation (Marchant, 1981).

Specific Influences

This section provides information on specific influences related to variations within the development of the family constellation.

The Special Sibling

A weak, sickly, handicapped, or retarded child may become "special." An exceptionally intelligent, gifted, or attractive child may also elicit an unusual amount of parental attention and invite dissatisfaction and dissension among siblings. An adopted child may also become "special" when treated by parents and siblings as a person in need of unique attention.

The Deceased Sibling

A deceased, stillborn, or miscarried child is frequently idealized by the family. Consequently, the next child born after such a death is in reality living with a preceding "ghost." Of course, it is difficult to compete with a "ghost." Moreover, the parents may become very overprotective afterwards and, in effect, try to wrap the next child in an emotional cotton batting. The child may choose to bask in such a stifling atmosphere, or may decide to rebel and strive for autonomy.

Family Losses

Losses of family members may change the constellation. The changes are often most severe when the losses occur early in the child's life. Losses usually have more dramatic effects if the family is small, if a greater imbalance of sex is left, or if other losses have also occurred. Of course, it is not so much the loss itself that creates the long-term difficulties as it is the individual's interpretations to those losses and resulting actions. As an example, juvenile delinquents and adult criminals are more likely than the general population to have lost members (especially their parents). Divorced couples are more likely than happily married couples to have experienced losses in early life.

Parents' Birth Order

The sibling position of the parents has a specific importance, especially for the only child. Generally, parents identify with the child in the family who matches their sibling position. Thus, the oldest boy may act like the youngest because the father was the youngest in his family of origin. The child also tends to identify with the same sex parent. This is especially true for the oldest or only child. And if parents feel disappointed because they have no son, sometimes a daughter will try to find favor through "tomboyish" behavior.

Sibling Competition and Rivalry

We all have some pleasant and some unpleasant thoughts and feelings about our brothers and sisters. We are likely to develop pleasant relationships when we satisfy one another's goals, desires, and values, and to develop unpleasant relationships when they clash. Since all children view their relationship with each brother and sister differently the relationship between any two of them is rather unique. While each child strives to find a place within the family, the other siblings carefully observe the means by which they succeed and fail.

Areas in which one child succeeds, the other often gives up; areas in which one child is weak and deficient, the other often advances and becomes strong and competent. Consequently, differences in temperament, interests, and abilities indicate competition between family members .

Competition between the first and second child is often very intense, stimulating each to move in opposite directions. Whatever field in which the first child has succeeded, the second considers taken, and thus seeks a different area. Each child yields the field to the more successful sibling and, in the discouragement, takes an opposite track.

Sometimes, however, the two keenest competitors display no open rivalry, but instead present a rather close-knit pair; nonetheless, their competitive striving is clearly revealed in personality differences. One may lead, being active, powerful, and protecting, while the other may follow, being passive, weak, and dependent. This is an instance in which intense competition does not interfere with mutual agreement, but instead allows each child to feel safe and secure in his or her particular area of striving. This arrangement is frequently seen in the case of twins in which one does the talking for the other to the point that the other's speech is actually developmentally delayed.

Parental Stimulation of Competition

Competition between or among siblings is further intensified when parents compare one child against another in an effort to stimulate each to greater efforts. Parents may openly or subtly encourage the children to work harder and achieve the parents' hoped for success. Such an approach often stimulates one child to completely avoid active participation in an area in which another sibling appears competent. Consequently, children close in age tend to "divide up" the territory in which they operate. If the first child is highly successful academically, the second tends to try something else such as becoming successful athletically or socially. Thus, in a highly competitive family, an "underachieving" child often has an "overachieving" sibling next door in the family constellation. Parents may not have "caused" this form of competition, but they almost always unwittingly contribute to it as do relatives, friends, neighbors, and teachers. This situation is a logical result of our highly competitive society.

Parental Expectations

Parents are frequently unaware of how their actions reinforce the child's interpretations of one's role with the family and community. For example, a "responsible" child is usually given more responsibility than other siblings. A "good" child frequently shows up the "bad" child by tattling, thus, emphasizing one's own good qualities in contrast—and the parents usually fall for it. A "real" boy or girl, "tomboy," "withdrawn" child, and "little" lady or gentleman are frequent labels given by parents and other adults, each with different implications. Consequently such children see themselves in these roles and live up to the expectations implicit in them.

Alliances

Similarity of attributes of siblings signifies alliances. In a family of four, for example, the first and third child and the second and fourth child usually form alliances. Alliance is indicated by the similar display of interests, behavior patterns, and attitudes. One parent may side with the child against the other parent as well as siblings siding with one another.

Age Differences

If there is a space of five or more years between children, each child will exhibit some of the attributes of an only child. The farther apart the children are in age, the more distant their relationship and the less influence they will likely have on one another. If there are two or more groups of children with a number of years existing between groups, they tend to cluster in subgroups with the leader having traits of the oldest with the other children having characteristics of the respective birth order positions. These subgroups can be referred to as separate families.

Oscar C. Christensen, Ed.D.

Sex Differences

The circumstances of an only girl among boys or an only boy among girls may present specific influences. Both girls and boys born in this position tend to develop to extremes—in either a masculine or feminine direction. Both boys and girls may feel somewhat isolated in this position within the family and have mixed feelings about their sex roles. Whichever role appears to be the most advantageous will be selected. Advantages or disadvantages are dependent on the family values placed on the different sex roles and the individual's perceived ability to live up to them. If both roles are valued and competition is minimal, they tend to get along harmoniously with the other sex. A boy among boys or a girl among girls often feels uncomfortable with the other sex and prefers the company of one's same sex.

Parental Favoritism

Parental favoritism can create very precarious circumstances, and such influences are best avoided, if at all possible. Alfred Adler supported this when he stated:

> *The dangers of favoritism can hardly be too dramatically put. Almost every discouragement in childhood springs from the feelings that someone is preferred.... Children are very sensitive and even a good child can take an entirely wrong direction in life through the suspicion that others are preferred* (Adler, 1956, p. 376).

Family Atmosphere

The family atmosphere is the characteristic or prevailing climate initiated and modeled by parents for children as a pattern of social living. It is the origin of the individual's values and attitudes (Missildine, 1955). The following are commonly observed family atmosphere that are presented by families in distress.

Overindulgence

In this atmosphere, the child is given endless presents, gifts, treats, and services of all kinds. The child: (1) often becomes bored, developing little initiative or persistence; (2) becomes passive, dependent, always asking "What's in it for me?" and more interested in getting than giving; and (3) may turn into a tyrant if the indulgence does not continue.

Overprotection

In this atmosphere, the parent overprotects the child and does not allow the child to venture out on one's own. The child: (1) often remains or becomes the "baby"—feeling small, weak, helpless, and irresponsible; (2) is often unable to function independently; (3) frequently tries to put others into personal service; (4) lacks self-confidence; and (5) may demand approval.

Oversubmission

In this atmosphere, the child's whims and demands are catered to. The child: (1) becomes the master, the "boss," with the parents becoming the slaves and servants; (2) demands more and more; (3) becomes impulsive; (4) demands through temper tantrums; and (5) has difficulty considering the needs or rights of others.

Pitying

In this atmosphere, the significance of minor aches and pains is exaggerated. Excessive pity is given to one who is disadvantaged due to a handicap, a loss, or misfortune. The child: (1) clings to this over-concern, using it to gain sympathy and to provide an excuse for passivity, non-participation, and non-contribution; (2) learns to expect special exemptions and privileges; and (3) becomes a "victim," seeing life as abusive, full of suffering, and tragedy.

Martyring

In this atmosphere, the martyring parents demonstrate the brutality of life and others. The child: (1) may become pessimistic, looking down on others who "caused" the suffering; (2) feels sorry, that "life is unfair"; (3) becomes self-righteously critical of others—in the name of "goodness"; and (4) learns to dominate and control others through "weakness."

Perfectionism

In this atmosphere, the child experiences a demanding parental attitude characterized by withholding approval until greater performance is achieved in accord with the parents' high standards. The child: (1) becomes overly serious and overly preoccupied with material, intellectual, or social achievements; (2) feels the need for constant and absolute success, and may strive endlessly and fruitlessly for it; (3) has an intense fear of failure and mistakes; (4) always "could have done better," and lives in an uphill struggle to be better; and (5) becomes discouraged about living up to parental expectations.

Oscar C. Christensen, Ed.D.

Competitive

In this atmosphere, the parents emphasize success and a high level of performance with each member creating one's own world and trying to out-do others. The child: (1) may be stimulated by such competition; (2) may also foster apprehension and feelings of complete failure; (3) may be further discouraged with feelings of hopelessness magnified by such competition; (4) may demonstrate a place within the family unit by becoming "the best at being the worst"; and (5) may become a "driver" and being almost exclusively concerned with personal success.

Materialistic

In this atmosphere, security is measured by what one owns or controls. The child: (1) may be unable to find the real joy of simple pleasures of life, (2) may lack inner resources and creativity; and (3) if also rebellious, may become strongly anti-materialistic.

Authoritarianism

In this atmosphere, the parents require absolute and unquestioned obedience. The child: (1) often rebels in later life or when free of the authority; (2) is likely to be inconsiderate of others, quarrelsome, unpopular, emotionally unstable, and/or very sensitive to praise and blame; (3) is polite, "respectful," and proper, but shy and timid; (4) is often unable to solve problems without the help of an authority; (5) often lacks creativity, spontaneity, and resourcefulness; (6) may resort to passive-aggressive strategies such as lying and stealing; and (7) frequently "goes wild" in an atmosphere of permissiveness.

Overcontrol

In this atmosphere, the child experiences constant parental coercion: supervision, direction, and redirection—an endless stream of anxious reminders. The child: (1) does not develop self-direction, but relies excessively on external direction; and (2) may assert independence passively by dawdling, daydreaming, forgetting, and procrastinating.

Suppressive

In this atmosphere, freedom to express genuine, honest thoughts and feelings is denied. The child: (1) learns to "put up a front," a facade, to avoid frequent reprimands and disapprovals; (2) may resort to daydreams and fantasies; and (3) learns to avoid close relationships, or has difficulty with intimate relationships.

Punitiveness

In this atmosphere, the parent's personal anger—rather than the child's error—usually determines the punishment. The child: (1) learns to "need" punishment—with such punishment creating the "need" for more punishment; and (2) may rebel with a revengeful attitude that will bring retaliation from the parent—retaliation begets retaliation begets retaliation. Anyone forcefully pushed down will seek to rise to a level of perceived equality.

Disparaging

In this atmosphere, the parents frequently and constantly criticize the child. The child: (1) may become doubtful of self-worth and overestimate the value of others; (2) may feel looked down on by others; (3) may become very critical to compensate for feelings of inferiority—a holier than thou attitude boosts one's own status by making others appear more worthless in comparison; (4) if active, may take the path of violent rebellion; (5) sometimes becomes the "scapegoat" of "the problem," drawing attention away from others' misbehavior or problems; and (6) may become cynical, critical, and pessimistic, lacking trust in self and others.

Inconsistent

In this atmosphere, parental discipline is erratic and routines, schedules, and structure are nonexistent. The child: (1) does not know what to expect of others or what others expect; (2) may develop a lack of trust, believing that life is arbitrary; (3) may become unstable, lacking self-control and motivation, becoming self-centered and craving excitement at almost anyone's expense; and (4) may demand variety and surprises as the rule, not the exception.

Neglecting

In this atmosphere, parental absence or preoccupation due to overwhelming problems, work, alcoholism, and drug addiction, divorce, or death are frequently seen. The child: (1) often lacks the capacity to form close, meaningful relationships; and (2) often develops low self-esteem and self-confidence.

Rejection

In this atmosphere, the child is rejected by the parents. Fortunately, absolute rejection, in which the child has no niche or acceptance within the family, is relatively rare. The child: (1) be-

Oscar C. Christensen, Ed.D.

comes bitter and anxious about apparent isolation and helplessness; (2) feels unacceptable, although this is not the case; and (3) may feel discouraged about self-worth.

Hopelessness

In this atmosphere, hopelessness, intense discouragement, and pessimism are prominent. The child: (1) feeling defeated sees little hope in future; and (2) is led to highly contagious pessimism (with innumerable real or imagined reasons for being that way).

Mutual Respect

This section has emphasized problematic family atmospheres that typically confront the Adlerian family counselor. In working with families the family counselor helps the family to create an atmosphere based in mutual respect.

In this atmosphere, the child is respected as a social equal by the parents. The child: (1) feels accepted; (2) feels that positive qualities are emphasized and that mistakes are minimized; (3) is trained for responsibility by being given responsibility according to ability; (4) experiences natural and logical consequences rather than rewards and punishments as means of discipline; (5) is encouraged by parents who recognize that misbehavior stems from discouragement rather than badness or evilness; (6) is encouraged to develop the courage to be imperfect; (7) is helped to develop a sense of humor; (8) observes the parents setting reasonable expectations and living up to them; (9) is exposed to honesty about feelings; (10) is treated courteously as a friend; (11) experiences warmth, affection, and love; (12) learns to be empathic—to see, hear, and feel things from the other's point of view; and (13) practices democracy in the home (Dewey, 1978).

Other Principles

There are other important principles that relate to the practice of Adlerian family counseling. These principles, including goal disclosure, are described in subsequent chapters on "The Family Counseling Process" and "Assessment in Adlerian Family Counseling," as well as in other texts (Dreikurs, 1959; Dinkmeyer & McKay, 1973).

As a final note, we believe in the importance of families having fun together. Playing together, as well as working together, leads to the kind of intimacy necessary for cooperation and cohesion. We suggest that Adlerian family counselors encourage playful interaction with the families they counsel as a means for developing an atmosphere of courageous imperfection.

References

Adler, A.A. (1956). *The individual psychology of Alfred Adler.* H.L. Ansbacher & R.R. Ansbacher (Eds.). New York: Basic Books.

Dewey, E.A. (1978). *Basic applications of Adlerian psychology for self-understanding and human relationships.* Coral Springs, FL: CMTI Press.

Dinkmeyer, D., & McKay, G.D. (1973). *Raising a responsible child: Practical steps to successful family relationships.* New York: Simon & Schuster.

Dreikurs, R. (1959). Fundamental principles of child guidance. In R. Dreikurs, R. Corsini, R. Lowe, & M. Sonskgaard (Eds.), *Adlerian family counseling: A manual for counseling centers.* Eugene, OR: The University of Oregon Press.

Dreikurs, R., & Soltz, V. (1964). *Children: The challenge.* New York: Hawthorn Books.

Dreikurs, R., Corsini, R., & Gould, S. (1975). *How to stop fighting with your kids.* New York: ACE Books.

Kelly, G.A. (1955). *The psychology of personal constructs* (Volume 1). New York: W.W. Norton.

Manaster, G.J., & Corsini, R.J. (1982). *Individual psychology: Theory and practice.* Itasca, IL: F.E. Peacock.

Marchant, W.C. (1981). Family forum. *Nevada Personnel and Guidance Journal, 2,* 130-133.

Missildine, W.H. (1955). *Your inner child of the past.* New York: Harper & Row.

Chapter 3

The Family Counseling Process

by Oscar C. Christensen
and
William C. Marchant

The science of human nature cannot be pursued with the sole purpose of developing occasional experts. Its proper goal is the understanding of human behavior by every human being, in as much as the power of self-knowledge and self-criticism lies within the scope of any intelligent adult (Adler, 1954, p. 21).

Alfred Adler first organized Child Guidance Clinics in Vienna after World War I. By 1930 his students and colleagues conducted thirty-two clinics in various locations throughout the city. There were, reportedly, similar clinics located throughout Germany and Hungary. All were discontinued by 1934 (Dreikurs, 1957).

With the prelude to World War II and the Nazi takeover of Europe, many prominent Adlerians, including Rudolf Dreikurs, were forced to flee the continent. Dreikurs immigrated to the United States and eventually settled in Chicago. By 1939, he had established a child guidance clinic at the Abraham Lincoln Center and the development of the open center family counseling model in the United States was begun.

In the mid 1950s, Ray Lowe and Oscar Christensen at the University of Oregon introduced open-center family counseling as a method of educating parents, children, and teachers in a College of Education setting.

The concept of family counseling as an educational endeavor, first advanced by Dreikurs and later amplified by Lowe, Christensen, and others, was the background for the development of a community parent-teacher education center movement The basic concept advanced was that the difficulties with children being experienced by parents and other adults was primarily due to lack of education, as opposed to the views of mental health professionals.

> *A much more optimistic concept of counseling could be one based not on illness but on health, not on abnormality but on normality. The model alluded to here is essentially an educational one, which makes the assumption that the lack of knowledge, information, or experience, rather than illness, is the basis of maladaptive behavior.*

> *While counselors, and indeed schools, are poorly equipped to cure illness, they are well designed to provide information, experiences, or education. It is assumed that people if provided new or pertinent information are capable of applying the new information to their situation, making the corrections necessary to bring about change* (Christensen, 1969, p. 12).

The educational model provided educators with a major breakthrough in coping with interpersonal relationship difficulties, which previously had been defined as illnesses and had thus remained the exclusive province of the medical profession. The proper domain of education is concerned with the eradication of ignorance. In situations where the difficulties experienced by adults with young people is a matter of lack of information, providing information is indeed an appropriate endeavor for educators. This concept provides educators with the impetus for the development of education centers in which parents, children, teachers, and concerned professionals can unite for the purpose of gaining and using new information, for the ultimate benefit of the child.

> *This rather optimistic construct is based largely on the Adlerian concept of man as a social being whose fundamental desire is to belong. Belonging is expressed in movement toward others The child's trial and error attempts a interpersonal movement may not always be socially acceptable and are subject to errors of*

perception and interpretation. As the child interprets or misinterprets his experiences with his inner and outer environments he draws conclusions about effective approaches to social living.

His attitude toward life in general constitutes his life style or life pattern, which is the key to the personality of each individual The concept of life style encompasses the unity of child's personality; all acts and attitudes are only facets of his general life style, which is based on his evaluation of himself and his ability. Maladjustment or maladaptive behavior is viewed as the expression of mistaken approaches to finding a place in the group or groups that encompass a child's life. As long as the child is not discouraged, he will seek his place through useful contributions appropriate to the demands of the situations; however, if he becomes discouraged in his attempt at social belonging, he switches to the use of compensatory or over-compensatory behavior, on the mistaken notion that this will ensure his acceptance. An implication for counseling with this conceptualization is, briefly, that the misbehavior of children is accounted for by their misinterpretations and mistaken concepts about themselves and the process of social living. If new information, designed to correct the mistaken self concept is adequately and meaningfully provided the child, he can, as a self-determining, creative human, effect self-change (Christensen, 1969, p. 12).

While the Adlerian model does permit and in fact provides for the private counseling of parents in an office, it is of great importance to recognize that the same process can take place with much broader impact, before an audience of parents and teachers. This process, in the eyes of many professionals, is one of Rudolf Dreikurs major contributions. It is estimated that the information provided for the family-in-focus is of value to eighty or ninety percent of the participating audience. Parents in attendance are able to make use of the information to some degree and do apply it directly to their family concerns. Based upon this assumption, the model is an extremely optimistic one, which accepts the fact that parents are capable of taking information gathered through observation and cognitive processes and translating it in terms of their own needs. Furthermore, that they are capable of applying the information to the resolution of problems within their own family. Some research is available which does indeed suggest this supposition to be valid: Essig (1971), Kamali (1967), Marchant (1972), Platt (1971).

Roles of Counselor as Educator

When counselors are viewed as teachers or educators, then each technique they can bring to bear that provides new information, insights, or learning to a parent or group of parents can be considered a valid counseling procedure. In many instances Dreikurs', Ginott's, Glasser's, and Gordon's child development books may be used constructively as counseling tools. Information supplied via reading is effectively utilized by a large percentage of the population.

For those parents who benefit most from an experiential approach, open-center counseling functions as a dynamic educational experience. The merit of a direct counseling experience for the family-in-focus is apparent, in that families are being provided with information explicitly related to their needs and concerns. Furthermore, members of the audience can be viewed as active participants in a realistic sense, since vicarious learning is available to them during the counseling sessions. In many instances it is as valid a learning experience as is direct intervention itself. For many parents it is an extremely valuable activity to sit in an audience and view another family in the process of problem resolution. The stress of participation is precluded by the fact that they are not directly involved. However, exposure is highly relevant since the concerns of one family are not that different from those of another. Expression of concerns may vary in form from family to family, but the dynamics involved are often extremely similar.

In the typical parent-teacher education center it is frequently found that parents and teachers will focus on the concerns of a given child. In many cases, not only are the parents interviewed by the counselor, but also the teacher of the child or children in question is involved in the interview. This offers multiple benefits to the child, the family-in-focus, and the audience. Inherent in this counseling situation is the possibility for improving community-school relationships through the process of demonstrating the importance of the school to the community through the open-center counseling approach. Often various special education or adjunct services of the school district can and do explain the purpose and functioning of their office through the parent education center. For example, if the family-in-focus has a child that is also involved in a special education, reading, or speech correction program, the special education teacher, the reading teacher, or the speech therapist is often part of the team that is approaching the resolution of the problems presented by the family. Through the process of the other expert acting as a consultant to the family counselor, the specialist also has the opportunity to explain the workings of specialized departments to the audience in attendance. One is encouraged by the ready cooperation of the various specialities with a parent-teacher education center (Christensen, 1972, p. 121).

The safeguards for the development of an open-centered process have an elegant simplicity and are relatively obvious. Primarily, counselors are validating their respect for the individual and the family by the assumption that they are not sick but that they simply lack information. This assumption alone accounts for the wide-scale acceptability of the parent-teacher education center model. The parents are not placed in the position of feeling that they are somehow sick, demented, or otherwise incapacitated. There is no particular stigma attached to being unaware; there is, however, a stigma attached to being sick. Another assumption that allows for a rather widespread participation is that people are capable of learning through educational experiences. This suggests something quite optimistic about people, which is reflected in their willingness to participate. The fact that no disturbed children are seen in the setting, only disturbing children, again reflects the further open nature of the process.

This view of children's behavior is of subtle yet powerful importance. If we see children as disturbed, we become involved in a circular process of mutual discouragement and eventual defeat. There is a finality to the word disturbed that reinforces our discouragement with the child, and with our ability to deal with that child. When we view children as disturbing, however, we recognize the interpersonal nature of relationships and are thus able to create more opportunities for successful counseling intervention.

Possibly the most dramatic statement of acceptability of the educational movement is that it is the epitome of accountability. Counselors are displaying their work in front of an audience, rather than hiding their skills behind a closed door. This may be regarded as accountability through visibility. If people can see what one does, there is less reason to question validity, assuming that what is observable has some element of face validity. Counselors are, in fact, substantiating their claims. They are working with the family in full view of the community with the probability of seeing the family at some point in the future. At a later time, people in the audience are able in retrospect to evaluate the effectiveness of the counseling progress since the first interview. This perhaps is the model's greatest strength, as the community can and does sit in evaluation of the counselor's proficiency and effectiveness in working with families.

Another assumption that must be made is that the child's educability is indeed the ultimate concern. An educator is justifiably involved in the education of the parent to improve the educability of the child or children involved. Any other vindication would take the process outside the realm of education. Educators are ultimately concerned with educating the child and the parent. This has proven to be of great benefit in improving the child's educational options. The assumption here is obviously that the child who appears at school with a minimum number of behavior problems, and is committed to being responsible for one's own behavior, is obviously most ready to accept the educational opportunities that the school has to offer.

It is the purpose of this chapter, therefore, to convey to the reader an operational model of the Adlerian family counseling process, with appropriate references to content. It is hoped that the use of flow charting techniques will increase the reader's understanding of Adlerian family counseling, as seen in Figure 1.

With reference to the flow chart as a graphic representation of the success, it is important at the outset to note a caution relative to the use of the chart. It is designed merely to clarify the counseling process and not to stultify it into a step-by-step regimented procedure.

Perhaps if the emphasis is put on the word flow in understanding the charting procedure, a correct interpretation will occur. That is, the counseling process should flow easily, smoothly, with a conversational naturalness. If we can understand the caution that the flow chart is merely an aid in clarifying the process, we may now turn to the counseling in some detail and attempt to develop some understanding of the elements of the counseling process. It would be very helpful if the reader attempting to understand the Adlerian family counseling process has previously viewed a demonstration of Adlerian family counseling. However, an excerpted typescript of such a demonstration will be included to use as an example in understanding the elements involved.

The first element in the counseling process, insofar as it is practiced in many counseling centers, is to establish the data base. The use of the data base as part of a record-keeping system is described more completely elsewhere (Marchant, 1972). However, suffice it to note here that data base information is all that data that is gathered about the family before the family counseling interview begins: such as identification data, the reason for referral to family counseling, and often the children's school reports, if an educational problem is indicated. This data is usually obtained during an intake interview prior to the appointment for counseling.

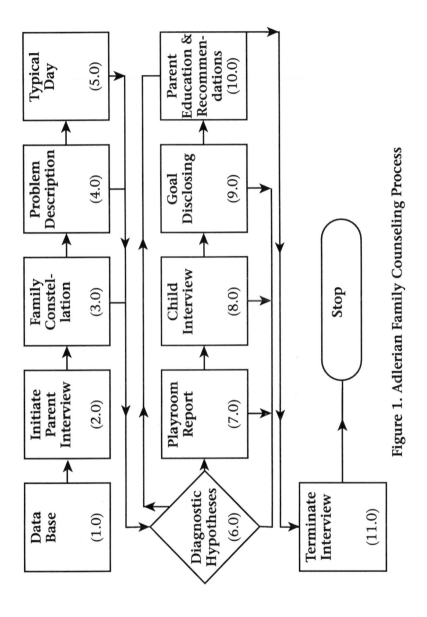

Figure 1. Adlerian Family Counseling Process

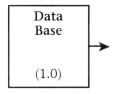

```
   Data
   Base

   (1.0)
```

After the data base information has been gathered, the family counseling interview usually commences with the interview involving the parents with the counselor. During the time that the parents are speaking with the counselor, the children are typically involved in freeplay activities under observation and supervision in a playroom, though this may not be the case in some private agency settings.

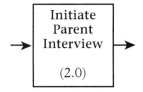

```
   Initiate
   Parent
   Interview

   (2.0)
```

Introduction	Explain Education	Explain Interaction as public	Explain Comonality as problems	
(2.1)	(2.2)	(2.3)	(2.4)	(2.0)

Several procedures have routinely been seen as very helpful in initiating a family counseling interview. Obviously, the kinds of introductions that are appropriate should be included at the outset. It is well to remember that the quality of the relationship that will exist during the family counseling can be developed most easily with an appropriate beginning At the start, the counselor has the opportunity to model the kinds of relaxed interactional procedures that should be the hallmark of each family interview. It has been helpful during most family counseling interviews, especially if conducted in an open-center setting, to explain the nature of the family education process involving the family-in-focus and an audience. Three important elements are seen to be quite appropriate as part of educating the parents to the nature of the counseling setting.

One element which seems to have a large impact on the family to be counseled is to explain to the family that the process that will occur is one of education, both for the family-in-focus and for the audience. The very notion of sharing information places the parents-in-focus in the position of giving help to others through their experience, rather than being solely a recipient of help. This has the effect of freeing the parents to be more open and honest about their concerns.

The *second* element which seems to be helpful in alleviating initial parental anxiety about having counseling occur in an open-center setting is an explanation of the nature of the data which will be involved in the family counseling process: that is, an explanation that the information which will be used during the family counseling setting is all based on interpersonal behavior; and interpersonal behavior by definition is public behavior. For example, the neighbors usually know that the parents scream at their children to come for supper, thus the implication of violation of confidentiality is avoided.

A *third* element that is very often helpful in alleviating anxieties which parents bring to the counseling setting is a short explanation of the commonality of problems experienced by parents. It should be emphasized that the reason for participating in the open-center session is to educate a larger group of parents, all of whom are probably experiencing similar problems in the area of adult-child relationships.

Counselor: (to audience) By way of getting started, let me point out to the audience, and through the audience the parents, the purpose of open-center family counseling. In the first place, this is really an educational experience, not only for the parents involved, but also for the audience. This observation arises from the assumption that parents concerns are similar from one family to the next, and that most parents who are having difficulties with their children are in need of new information as to how to deal with the children. Since the concerns are similar, at least in underlying dynamics, the presence of change for one family is similar to another family. I believe this attitude shows a great deal of respect for the families involved, because it must assume that parents are intelligent and caring people who will make the final choice as to whether or not to use the information they receive here.

One ground rule—the audience is encouraged to participate in the counseling discussion as long as the focus of
your questions and comments are directed toward this
family. If you want to ask a question about your family,
then you must arrange to be the family-in-focus.

Okay? Then let's get started.

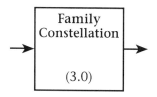

The initial step in information gathering which occurs between
the counselor and the parents is establishing of the family constellation information.

Birth Order	Miscarriages Stillbirths	Serious Childhood Illness	Others in Family	
(3.1)	(3.2)	(3.3)	(3.4)	(3.0)

Four basic kinds of information are involved here: the first piece
of information is the birth order, that is, the names and ages of the
children in the family. One should at this time determine if there
have been any miscarriages or stillbirths and where they occurred,
as occurrence of miscarriage or stillbirth might affect the way in
which a parent relates to the remaining children; it is sometimes
helpful to inquire if any serious childhood illness has been present,
such as rheumatic fever, polio, chicken pox, and so forth. One
should also inquire if there are others living in the home, such as
grandparents, uncles, aunts, boarders, foster children, and so on.
The use to which one puts this information is very important.

An excellent way of cementing the relationship between the
counselor and the parent which has been used quite effectively by
many family counselors is for the counselor at this point to build
some hypothesis and guess as to the behavioral characteristics of
the children in the family. This tends to help the relationship from
the standpoint of demonstrating to the family that the counselor

has some understanding of family process which might be helpful for this particular family. A second use for this information is merely the development of initial diagnostic hypotheses about the dynamics of the family relationships. As noted on the flow chart sheet, this is an initial point for the development for such an hypothesis. It should be emphasized that at this point in time hypotheses are very tentative, subject to modification or confirmation based upon additional data gathered. If one does not feel that a sufficient background of information is available to develop diagnostic hypothesis, based upon the family constellation information, the following reading is recommended: Dreikurs, Grunwald, & Pepper (1971).

Counselor: Let me introduce Maxine Newlon who is the parent in our family-in-focus today. Maxine, would you tell the audience the names and ages of your children?

Maxine: I am one of those fortunate or maybe unfortunate mothers who has twins. Age 6, Mary Ann and John.

Counselor: There are two guesses one can make about twins: one seems to always know which one was born first, and two, that the first born will assume most of the characteristics of the typical eldest child and in a typical, non-twin constellation. Mary Ann is not only the elder twin but also a girl, which gives her a distinct probability of being the most perfectionistic, not necessarily the best—but the one who worries more about "doing things right." This could be a handicap in that it sometimes produces an acute fear of failure, that makes it dangerous for the child to try anything new.

Maxine: Mary Ann is talkative and very active. She doesn't know what being quiet is like unless she's asleep. She doesn't do very well in school. Both are pretty good about keeping their rooms.

Maxine: John is quietly shy and does very well in school. In behavior, both the same. They fight with each other and other children, but the two stick up for each other.

Maxine: Mary Ann doesn't think she can do very well in school. She says I can't do this, I don't know how. I tell her she has to try first before she knows that, and then we'll help if she can't, and then of course, we'll help. An example might be while reading a book, she comes to a word she has had before and she doesn't know it. I'll say, "Well, sound it out." She goes through the word till she almost has it and then she says, "Oh, I just can't." Then I usually get angry.

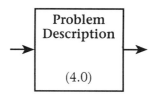

Problem Description
(4.0)

After the family constellation information is developed, the counselor can begin immediately to identify the problems involved from the viewpoint of the parents.

Identify Problems	Describe Problem(s)	Obtain Specific Example	Establish Parental Response	
(4.1)	(4.2)	(4.3)	(4.4)	(4.0)

Very often this problem description phase begins with establishing the identity of the child about whom the parents are currently most concerned. Once the identity of that child has been established, the parents should be asked to describe the kinds of concerns they have about the problem child and, most important, should be asked to recite specific examples of each of these concerns. One cannot emphasize too much the importance of eliciting examples—specific incidents—in which the parents have been involved in a disturbing situation with the child. During the process of having the parents describe the specific example, it is most important for the counselor to inquire about how the parent responds to that situation. ("And what do you do?")

In order to emphasize the interpersonal nature of the conflict situation in the family it is very important to have the parents understand their contribution to that interpersonal situation. Therefore, establishing what the parent does or how the parent responds is very important from the standpoint of helping the parents to understand that they contribute to the situation as well as help the counselor to more completely understand the interpersonal dynamics of the family.

Establishing a second kind of parental response is most important while specific situations are being described. The parents should be asked how the child's action made the parent feel, that is, what was the emotional response of the parent. This is important in helping the counselor to understand the goal of the child in the situation involved. The process of understanding the four goals of misbehavior is more completely described in brief later in this chapter. Again it should be emphasized that during the problem description process, the counselor should be developing hypotheses about the dynamics of the family. Experienced counselors will oftentimes feel comfortable in sharing their diagnostic guesses with the parents just after the interview.

Counselor: We can already see one of the dynamics involved in this. Not being able to do something—working to get Mother to help her do it. This leads me to speculate—to build an initial hypothesis based on the response that Mom gets angry. Assuming that her behavior has purpose, the best test is the impact of the child's behavior on the adult assisting her. What better way to keep Mom entwined with her? I think she may be demonstrating this. Mom, when she says that last part, do you ever feel she is using you? Therefore the anger?

Mother: Yes.

Counselor: This has the probability of reinforcing her for not knowing the word. In effect, you are teaching her not to learn. Any other behaviors that you might tell us about?

Mother: With a toy, she first throws it down, then picks it up and brings it to me and I show her how to work it, then she keeps bringing it back to me and I finally say, "Forget it, I'm not going to help you any more." She then goes away.

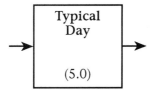

Having the parents describe a typical day in their household is usually helpful in understanding the total home situation. It is also very valuable when working in a family counseling setting to help the audience understand the dynamics of the parent-child relationship. It is oftentimes during the description of the typical day that the counselor gathers the most important information relative to confirming the initial diagnostic guesses that have been developed.

The flow chart lists some of the questions that can be asked in an effort to get an understanding of the families total situation (Figure 2). It should be emphasized that it is not necessary to ploddingly go through each of the questions listed in the flow chart. One need only gather the amount of information necessary to confirm or refute one's hypothesis about the various qualities of the family relationship. It has been the experience of many family counselor educators to have beginning students gather in great detail information about the family's typical day, and yet know practically no more about the interpersonal dynamics involved than they did before the information was gathered. What is being emphasized here is that each piece of information should be evaluated to see if it is consistent with the meaning of previously gathered information. For example, if one child in the home consistently gets up very early in the morning and always runs to get into bed with the parents, this might have a quite different meaning from that of the child who gets up first, goes quietly into another room, and plays by oneself.

It is important throughout the description of the typical day to again get the parents to describe their responses to the various situations. One should ask both parents, "How do you respond behaviorally and how do you respond emotionally in each of the specific situations described?" Again, this helps to confirm or refute hypotheses previously made about the dynamics of the family. While the flow chart indicates the more chronological relationship of each event to another, it might be pointed out that mealtime problems can occur at each of three meals throughout the day as opposed to just the evening.

It can also point out that household chores may occur at various times throughout the day, and information about successful completion of household chores may be asked at any time during the family counseling interview. The box 5.14 on household chores in the flow chart is included at that point merely as a convenience for the person learning family counseling.

It is often quite important during the process of gathering further information about the typical day for the counselor to have a skillful recorder present to keep a record of the information gathered during this part of the interview. Frequently, several kinds of problems become apparent during information gathering about a typical day that have not previously been alluded to by the parents. At some future time in the family counseling relationship, these problems might be dealt with by the counselor. Strategies for their resolution may then be devised.

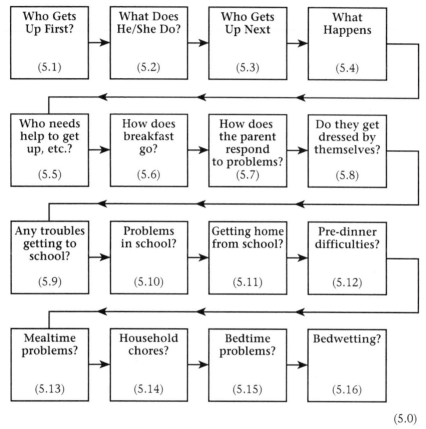

Figure 2. The Typical Day

Counselor: Let's look at a typical day.

Mother: I have to get them both up. I normally turn on the light and say, "It's time to get up." Then I get the other one from the other room. They'll sometimes say, "I don't want to get up this early." They usually take turns saying this. Last night Mary Ann was afraid, so she went and got in bed with John. I told them to get up and in a little while she's back in her bed. I told her to get up. She said, "I'm too tired and I don't want to go to school."

Counselor: What about John?

Mother: His room is too close to ours and he doesn't want to hear from his father which means a lot of hollering. They then have breakfast and take out the garbage and dust and then they have to get to the bus. Yesterday Mary Ann forgot dusting because I forgot it.

Counselor: Whose responsibility is it?

Mother: It's hers.

Counselor: But who is responsible to remind her?

Mother: Mine, so I guess I am responsible.

Counselor: As long as you accept the responsibility for them, they are not really being responsible. How does breakfast go?

Mother: Breakfast goes fine. If they have a fight it is between themselves. They dress and watch the clock.

Counselor: So they are showing that they really do take on a lot of responsibility. Some parents have to walk them to the bus.

Mother: They like to go to school.

Counselor: Yes, children usually like school. Typically, there are more people to bug at school!

Mother: John gets stars on his papers at school. When he brought a paper home with no star on it, he stood in the corner. He takes his punishment pretty well when he know's he's been wrong. Mary Ann's report card shows that she doesn't pay attention. She doesn't leave the other kids alone, likes to be the center of attention, talks, pokes children, then teacher pays attention to her.

Counselor: There are two ways of being best. One is by being best at being best, other is by being best at being worst at school. It's a status position. If you can't be one, be the other. It isn't bad, it is simply nonproductive. She is not learning what she needs to learn.

Counselor: What about after school?

Mother: In the evening they have a snack and then do what they have missed in the morning.

Counselor: How do they react to that?

Mother: They grumble about it, but they do it. They say, "Why do I always have to do all this?" I say, "I'm sorry, I have to wash all your clothes too, but I'm not crying." This usually happens if they have had a bad day at school.

Counselor: How do they get along with other kids in the neighborhood?

Mother: There are no other kids to get along with. They have each other. Sometimes they get tired of each other and fight.

Counselor: Tell us about their last fight. When did it occur?

Mother: Just before we came today. John would say something and Mary Ann began repeating everything he had said. I asked her to stop. He called her names. I got the flyswatter and it stopped. Our living room is set up for quiet or watching TV. They have their bedrooms to play or fight in.

Counselor: Uh huh. Rules are made to violate and therefore to get involvement of the parents.

Mother: If they won't go out, I let them go ahead and fight in their rooms.

Counselor: Does the flyswatter really help? No, not really, but it makes Mother feel a little better at the time. What we often teach is how to be better at what they are doing. I'll teach you to hit people, as we hit them. As we hit them, we teach them to use hitting as a way of solving problems. If we abuse children, we teach them to abuse others. If spanking really helped, we d have a lot of well-adjusted people in the world. Children who respond to spanking typically don't need it, and those who do need spanking usually aren't affected by it. Further, once spanked, the child is no longer responsible for one's behavior. I tend to disregard the value of spanking. If you leave them alone, the fighting stops. They like the noise and want other people to holler, becoming part of the fight. They are extremely effective in getting others involved. When you interfere, what words do you use?

Mother: I ask them to stop and I tell them to stop. If they don't do that, I get up and help them down the hall to their room.

Counselor: Why don't we just save energy? Cut out the first two steps.... Just get up and help them down the hall. I have the suspicion this mother is like most of us. We gradually get madder, and when mad enough, get up and do something about it. It's the old chicken and egg idea—whether motion or emotion comes first.

Counselor: From my point of view, emotion grows out of motion, so give your energy to get up and do it. When Mom gets mad, she now has the energy to get up out of her easy chair and take them down the hall. What would happen if you just aimed them down the hall?

Mother: They would be surprised if I took them down the hall.

Counselor: They'd be shocked! They didn't get Mother upset.

Mother: Sometimes they quit.

Counselor: How long before you get involved?

Mother: When one starts hollering.

Counselor: Mother has been trained to respond after the fight has been escalated to the hollering stage.

Mother: They show me their scratches. I don't pay much attention to them.

Counselor: What if it were two stitches?

Mother: I'd be very unhappy.

Counselor: Would it make you angry at the stitcher or the stitchee?

Mother: The one who did the job.

Counselor: My own interpretation is that both children are equally involved. Which child is the good guy?

Mother: I'd say its about 50–50.

Counselor: Yell at both of them together, with information we could tell Mother that she cannot play judge.

Mother: I've been telling them I'm not a referee.

Counselor: Good! I'm guessing that there is a relationship between fighting and reading. Who wins the fights?

Mother: Mary Ann usually gets the better of him. To show me he's hurt, John puts his hand up to his neck and wants me to ask him what's wrong. I'll say, "It's pretty bad, isn't it? I guess it's what you get when you fight."

Counselor: And how do you feel when he comes crying?

Mother: Angry, and I also feel sorry for him, but then, he deserved it! Also, why couldn't it be Mary Ann who loses once in a while?

Counselor: It sounds to me that you feel defeated, that you can win. They are the bosses and you lose. This would lead to a firmer hypothesis of a power struggle between you and your children. They cooperate to defeat you.

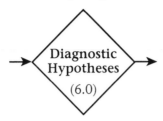

Usually at this point in time the counselor has developed some very strong guesses about the kinds of interpersonal processes that are occurring in the family. Often it is very helpful to share these guesses with the parents before one interviews the children. The typical guesses usually involve the goal of misbehavior utilized by children in the direction of the significant adult. They are included for consideration here as a subsystem in the flow chart.

Attention Getting	Power	Revenge	Assumed Disability	Other Excitement, etc.	
(6.1)	(6.2)	(6.3)	(6.4)	(6.5)	(6.0)

The parent interview usually terminates at this point, and while the parents are leaving the counseling room, the counselor may be interested in hearing a report from the playroom on the activities of the children while they were in the playroom. The work of the playroom worker has been described elsewhere (Dreikurs et al., 1959). Most likely the individual counselor will be able to suggest to the playroom personnel the kind of information which is most appropriate for the setting. For example, one might be interested in the child's interaction with the adults in the playroom as well as the interactions with other children in the playroom situation. Often, playroom situations can be developed in which a situation is structured involving the playroom supervisor in a planned situation with the child to see how the child responds to that adult's suggestions, and so on. Such information can be helpful in understanding if the child is relating consistently to all adults in one's life space or involved at different levels with different adults.

Observer: Mary Ann and John came in together, and stayed pretty close to each other for the first ten minutes. They played cooperatively for a time and then elected to go their separate ways. Both interacted easily with the other children and both occasionally demanded adult interaction. Mary Ann, by asking someone to help her figure out a game (which she had been observed playing previously) and John, by showing the playroom worker a picture he had been working on.

Counselor: This rather supports Mother's description of the children. Mary Ann used her inability or weakness as a means of being powerful. John used success and accomplishment as his method of involving adults.

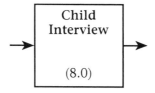

After the playroom report has been completed, the children enter the room for the child interview. It is most helpful to begin gathering information about the sibling interrelationships as soon as the children enter the room: how each individual child enters the room; which child helps another child, or which child needs help to find one's way to the appropriate chairs; is there running, pushing and shoving to get into different chairs; this is all very helpful information in understanding the relationships existing among the children. Very often this kind of information is much more explicit in educating the audience than is the information elicited during the verbal portions of the counselor-child interview.

Different counselors will develop different styles of interacting with children. It is important for several characteristics to be present during the interview with the children. Also, it is important to note that the interview with children is not the time in which the counselor should waste large amounts of energy in discussions on information not germane to the immediate task at hand. For example, discussions of the child's impression of the weather might be helpful to get the counselor to relax, but is seldom helpful to the child. Children are fully aware that they are present in a contrived situation. More important than discussions of irrelevant material at this point is the counselor's demonstration that the situation in which they are meeting is a contrived situation for the purpose of helping people learn about families.

Usually the early steps involved in talking with the children are to share with the child the concerns, as they have been enumerated by the parent. It is important to note that the counselor is not conducting an inquisition during the child interview to determine if mother or father or child is offering the most correct description offered, because what is most important is not the facts as they are presented but the individual's interpretation of those facts. Thus, the counselor is trying to arrive at some understanding of each individual's perception of one's present situation. If the counselor were to say, for example, "Mom tells me that you guys fight a lot" and one of the children were to respond, "No, we don't fight," the counselor could then say, "Well, Mom's concerned about your fighting." The next counselor's inquiry would be, "Why is it do you suppose that you fight so much?" At this point the counselor is trying to develop the process of goal disclosure.

Counselor: (to children) Thank you for coming—do you know why you are here?

Children: No... Mother brought us....

Counselor: Well let me explain a bit then. This is a group of parents and teachers and we are here to learn about how families can live together better. Mother has been helping us and now it's your turn. Mom tells us you two fight a lot. How do your fights get started?

Mary Ann: He starts saying things and I start copying him.

Counselor: That's a good way all right. How come you start fighting?

John: Because she wants to fight and I fight with her.

The goal disclosure process very often sounds quite stilted to one not skilled in its use. The most important characteristic of disclosing the child's goal is that the disclosure should be suggestive, not accusatory. That is, the counselor is merely sharing a guess about the child's motivation in this particular situation. In the case of the fighting example from the previous paragraph, the counselor might inquire, "Do you know why you fight so much?" To which the child may reply with a variety of answers, all of which are acceptable. The counselor can respond, "You may be right but could there be another reason involved?" The counselor might then ask, "Do you mind if I guess what another reason for your fighting might be?" And here is the most important part of the goal disclosure when the counselor asks, "Could it be that you guys are fighting just to show Mom who's boss?" The importance in being speculative in each of the inquiries is that it is very likely that the counselor will be wrong with the initial guess. And it is much easier to modify the guess than to modify an accusatory statement or statement of absolute fact. The conversational nature of the interview is more easily maintained, and the counselor is free to make additional guesses if the initial guess is incorrect.

After the counselor has shared with the children the counselor's hypothesis about what is going on in the family, it is often appropriate to share with the children the kinds of recommendations that will be made to the parents. This is usually done in a somewhat more general way than with the detail in which the recommendation will be conveyed to the parent.

Counselor: I could be wrong but could fighting be another way of keeping Mother busy?

John: Yep!

Counselor: Or, is it to show Mom who is boss, do you think?

Mary Ann: You read my mind!

Counselor: Oh, I doubt that, but it was a good guess I think.

Mary Ann: It's funnier to do that.

Counselor: Another thing, when you are reading in the evening and come to a word you've had before, what happens?

Mary Ann: I talk. I say I don't know it.

Counselor: Did you know it the day before?

Mary Ann: I'm not sure about if I knew it yesterday.

Counselor: What happens at school when reading with your teacher?

Mary Ann: She makes me do it. One day she made me put my head down. I make her mad easy.

Counselor: How does Dad do it?

Mary Ann: He makes me stay up till its done. Some take some time. Probably an hour.

Counselor: Why do you suppose you don't know how to read the words?

Mary Ann: Because of talking and not paying attention to the word.

Counselor: Do you think it may possibly be a way of keeping teacher busy (no response) or possibly showing how powerful you are? (recognition reflex, slight smile).

Mary Ann: Mrs. Hendricks takes it easy on me sometimes. When she yells at me I feel scared. When I'm scared I follow along and pay attention.

Counselor: Do you think that's why she yells at you?

Mary Ann: When I don't follow along and pay attention you get "meaner," that's what I told my teacher.

Counselor: If you pay attention and follow along she won't get mad. When she gets mad that's when you know she's paying attention to you?

Mary Ann: I have to, if I don't know the words.

Counselor: Is this your way of making Mother mad at you? This may be a way that you're powerful. You're pretty good at it too. How are you getting along at school John, any troubles?

John: Fighting at school. Teacher tells me to stay in for a week and I got to go out on recess because another kid was bothering me. When I was five years old I could fight first graders.

Counselor: Pretty good fighter, eh?

Mary Ann: To me he is. I can whip him, the same way Mama does—with a flyswatter.

John: I fought with first graders and teacher told me to come in and then go back to our desk for a rest period.

Counselor: I wonder if there might be some other way to handle situations like that.

Mary Ann: Give up.

Counselor: Yes, that's one way.

Mary Ann: Sometimes I never give up.

Counselor: I know it. Sometimes you can't give up. You are teaching us very much what it's like to be children, being powerful is necessary.

Mary Ann: I have four ways of being better than John: flyswatter, belt, telling Mother, and number four, I get to kick him.

Counselor: Sometimes you think you're better for being worse than John?

Mary Ann: That is true.

Counselor: I think this may be because you are so worried about being different from John. When is the last time you told Mary Ann you like her, John? Why don't you tell her now. (He did.)

Mary Ann: I kinda like him, too. He's cute.

Counselor: Do you know why he doesn't tell you how good you are?

Mary Ann: He's a scaredy cat?

Counselor: If he tells you how good you are, it might make him look worse. He has to learn that he doesn't have to be better than you. You are both good enough. You've been trying to be different from John because you didn't think you could be as good as he is. I think you are.

John: Once Mother went to school and my teacher said I was being good and Mom told my Dad and he said, "Good," and the next day I went to school and Mike was bothering me and I smacked him in the face. I got in trouble.

Counselor: Some of the family values are shown: being powerful, being boss, being right. We appreciate your being here and hope you'll come back to see us.

Mary Ann: Mom already told us we would come back.

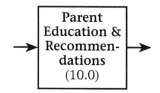

Parent
Education &
Recommen-
dations
(10.0)

After the child interview is terminated and the children have gone back to the playroom, the parents return for the parent education and recommendation portion. This is the time when the counselor shares the conclusions about the dynamics of the family in terms of providing a new understanding of the family situation to the parents. During this time, the parents and counselor, perhaps with the aid of individuals in the audience, determine the recommendations to be made for the family. Specifically, after an initial interview the family is usually given one or two tasks on which to work for the coming one or two-week period. Usually it is best not to inundate the family with more recommendations than they are able to implement during the short period of time before the next counseling interview. It is also important that the family achieve success with the initial recommendations so they will be encouraged to implement additional recommendations after future interviews.

Counselor: It's pretty clear that the fighting is designed to keep Mom busy, but the reading seems to be for power. "You can't make me do that." You and Mary Ann fighting, you and your husband are probably both pretty good at being boss.

Mother: I suspect so. . . . Yes.

Counselor: John is showing power more overtly, being right. While Mary Ann is passive. "I'm helpless, you have to help me." I might suggest that rather than getting hung up on a word, enjoy the story and say the word quietly and unemotionally, and not get into a fight with her. By not getting caught up in being right, Mary Ann and you can have a pleasant reading experience. Would our reading specialist agree?

Specialist: (in the audience) Oh, absolutely.

Counselor: I can't be an expert in all things, so I often ask for opinions of others who are the experts. When fighting occurs, I would suggest you remove yourself from the scene. Simply don't worry about the noise. You might have to physically leave the scene, have coffee with a neighbor, or take a walk. Don't pay any attention, if it means wearing a stereo headset, whatever it takes to be truly out of the action. You need to take a look at Mary Ann in the perspective of the new information you have gotten today—when we don't think we're very good, at least we have to think the other person is worse.

Mother: She'll ask why when I ask her to do something. I say because I asked you to and I want you to and you will be a lot of help to me.

Counselor: You finally got to a good reason after the third try.

Mother: I tell her because you .are going to your room that's why, and I don't want to discuss it any more.

Counselor: By the time you get to the part about going to your room, how do you feel?

Mother: Very upset.

Counselor: Almost angry, if you permitted yourself to be angry?

Mother: Yes.

Counselor: Her purpose is to keep people in continuous contact or communication. What times do you have alone with her to just talk?

Mother: She helps me with the dishes. She washes the dishes and stands there and just talks, all the time, never giving you a chance to talk.

Counselor: She is over-demanding, making Mother exclusively hers.

Counselor: What does she talk about?

Mother: Oh, about the dishes or anything. Another time is doing the grocery list and while putting the clothes away. She checks the list.

Counselor: You might try saying, "You write the list and I'll check it." If she doesn't know the word, tell her to draw a picture of it. Symbolic language.

Oscar C. Christensen, Ed.D.

Mother: When I go to the store they usually go with me and help me push the cart.

Counselor: How about your becoming the cart pusher and letting them find the groceries for you?

Mother: They might break something. They usually do.

Counselor: I've found the safest thing with a little one is to pick up ten pounds of sugar and give it to him to carry. By giving a kid responsibility, it's like spitting in her soup. She'll eat it, but not enjoy it so much. By showing that they can learn to read labels, that may say, "Look at this, you just can't fool me about being unable to read!"

Mother: One of the teachers sent home a list of words and she looked at it and said, "Could it be. . . ?" I'd say, "Yes." She knew what they were.

Counselor: Label things such as a box with candy in it. A "non-hearing" child test is to say softly, "Do you want some candy?" and they'll come from blocks around. They are not non-hearing but mother-deaf. Demonstrate to her that she's already reading, already able to find things. Then you can say, "I'm sorry, I won't accept that you are a non-reader." Teachers can adapt this. What does John do when Mary Ann is having trouble with words?

Mother: Sometimes helps, sometimes says, "I'm not going to help you any more." She'll say, "I'm sorry, I won't do it any more" and he does help her.

Counselor: A con artist. What does she do that she could teach John? Does he ever help with the dishes?

Mother: No. He doesn't care to. Sometimes they do it by themselves and there is water all over the place.

Mother: They clean it up, but it is just seeing the mess. It's right there!

Counselor: No, you are right, they're being upset. Couldn't you phrase it so she could teach him to help clean up? A child who is the receiver of help needs to be the giver of help. This might have payoffs for Mary Ann at school, also. Going to kindergarten across the way to teach reading.

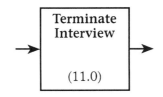

After the recommendations are completed the interview is terminated and arrangements are made for follow-up interviews as are necessary.

Counselor: It is time to quit—let's review what it is you're going to do this next week before we see you again.

Mother: Well. . . I'm going to try to stay out of their fights.

Counselor: How does one try to stay out of fights? It seems to me you either decide to get involved, or you decide to stay out of their fights. Which will it be?

Mother: Then I'll stay out!

Counselor: How?

Mother: . . . even if I have to take a walk.

Counselor: What about the reading?

The typical pattern of counseling would be to see the family every two weeks over an eight or ten-week time period. One agreement is that the parents participate as part of the audience those weeks when they are not the family-in-focus. Parents frequently report that many of the ideas presented during counseling become much more vivid while observing other families being counseled.

Since the concept of process is basically educational, the counselor can also be viewed as a learner. It is not false humility to state that the counselors are in a constant process of learning from the families they counsel.

The audience is also a source of extremely valuable assistance, both to the counselor and the family-in-focus. The report of an audience parent, as to how a particular principle was implemented and its results, is most frequently the turning point for the parents to attempt a change themselves. Parents often accept the credibility of another parent whereas the counselor may be suspect. Another value of the audience is to monitor the counselor. Audience agreement with the counselor's recommendation enhances the probability of the recommendation being carried out. Audience disagreement requires the counselor to reevaluate and either explain the purpose of the recommendation more clearly or disregard the recommendation entirely and develop a more appropriate course of action.

Adlerian open-center family counseling represents a valid parent educational tool, which employs a sound theoretical basis, valid teaching techniques, and appropriate counseling methods. It is accurately classed as a group counseling method and one which can transmit information to the public largely because of its common sense approach and rejection of esoteric language.

The Adlerian model of family counseling provides a potentially powerful vehicle for educating large numbers of parents and teachers. Until accurate psychological information is available to the general population, efforts in the mental health field will be inadequate in meeting the needs. Change will occur on a broad level only when mental health professionals share their knowledge with society on a preventative basis. Then Adler's goal will be accomplished: the understanding of human behavior by every human being.

References

Adler, A. (1954). *Understanding human nature.* Greenwich, CT: Fawcett.

Christensen, O.C. (1969). Education: A model for counseling in the elementary school. *Elementary School Guidance and Counseling, 4*(1), 12-19.

Christensen, O.C. (1972). Family education: A model for consultation. *Elementary School Guidance and Counseling, 7*(2),121-129.

Dinkmeyer, D., & Sherman, R. (1989). Brief Adlerian family therapy. *Individual Psychology: The Journal of Adlerian Theory, Research, and Practice, 45* (12), 148-158.

Dreikurs, R. (1957). Our child guidance clinics in Chicago. *Collected papers of Rudolf Dreikurs.* Eugene, OR: University of Oregon Press.

Dreikurs, R., Corsini, R., Lowe, R., & Sonstegard, M. (Eds.). (1959). *Adlerian family counseling.* Eugene, OR: University of Oregon Press.

Dreikurs, R., Grunwald, B., & Pepper, F.C. (1971). *Maintaining sanity in the classroom* (second edition). New York: Harper & Row.

Essig, J.D. (1971). *Prediction accuracy as a method of evaluating the Adlerian approach to improving family adjustment.* Unpublished doctoral thesis, University of Arizona.

Grunwald, B., & McAbee, H. (1985). *Guiding the family.* Muncie, IN: Accelerated Development.

Kamali, R.M. (1967). *A study of the effectiveness of counseling in a community parent-teacher education center.* Unpublished doctoral thesis, University of Oregon.

Marchant, W.C. (1972). Counseling and/or consultation: A test of the education model in the elementary school. *Elementary School Guidance and Counseling, 7*(1), 48.

Platt, J. (1971). Efficacy of the Adlerian model in elementary school counseling. *Elementary School Guidance and Counseling, 6*(2), 86-91.

Sherman, R., & Dinkmeyer, D. (1987). *Systems of family therapy: An Adlerian integration.* New York: Brunner/Mazel.

Sweeney, T.M. (1989). *Adlerian counseling.* Muncie, IN: Accelerated Development.

Chapter 4

Stepfamilies

by Lynn O'Hern-Hall
and Frank Williams

To marry a second time represents a triumph of hope over experience.
Samuel Johnson (1709-1784)

The make-up of families in our society is rapidly changing. One of these major changes is the increase of stepfamilies. In 1980, 41% of all marriages contracted involved at least one partner who had been married previously. Over one-half of these previously married persons had children. In 1978 an estimated 6.5 million children under the age of 18 (or 10.2% of all children under 18) were living with a biological parent and stepparent. Four out of five persons who divorce remarry within three years after the divorce is final. The decade of the 70s marked the first time in which remarriage subsequent to divorce, instead of death, was the norm.

Assuming that the current level of divorce will not decline, the probability that an individual will participate in a reconstituted family either while growing up (in one's family of origin) or as an adult (in one's family of procreation) is undoubtedly close to, if not greater than, one in two. Add to this the chances that this hypothetical person will be involved in divorce and remarriage as a grandparent (not to mention as an uncle, aunt, niece, nephew, or cousin) and it becomes evident that almost no one born today will be denied membership in a reconstituted family (Furstenberg, 1980, p. 458).

What's in a Name?

One can immediately begin to see how problems might arise. A major issue in working with and learning about stepfamilies is what to call them. In the literature such words as reconstituted, remarried, synergistic, instant family, amalgamated, binocular, and blended are all used with a little different meaning each time. John Visher (1981) suggested that

> . . . *none of the attempts to coin euphemistic substitutes for stepfamilies appear to have the advantage of describing a family unit which includes all equally—the remarried parent, the stepparent and all of the children who are simultaneously children of one of the couples and stepchildren of the other, or a child of both* (p. 2).

> *He continues to say that "calling this family unit a stepfamily is clear and descriptive without any attempt to conceal or obscure the relationships within the family" (p. 2). As we will see later, stepfamilies, by their nature, are confusing and difficult to understand. Having to use different words to explain each variation increases that confusion. For this chapter, the word "stepfamily" will be used to mean any family in which there is at least one adult in the role of stepparent, whether the children are living in the same house or not.*

> *Many combinations of people and roles are in included in the definition of stepfamilies. The two most frequent are the biological parent with children and the stepparent, or the biological parent with children and a stepparent with children. But within these combinations, other possibilities exist such as children residing outside the home, adults who have never married or are childless, parents with adult children, and children living in two different homes. A can be seen, the family is not easy to define and is very confusing to understand—but they are all stepfamilies!*

> *Another confusion centers around what everyone should call each other. If being in a stepfamily is perceived as negative, the family may attempt to hide it by forcing children to call the stepparent either Mom or Dad—many times creating loyalty confusion. However, there are instances, after a death or desertion of a parent, when the label of Mom or Dad comes naturally and is therefore very legitimate term. At first, no one knows what*

Oscar C. Christensen, Ed.D.

to do about introductions, what to call one another, or even how to talk to one another. *One four-year-old boy, while playing in the yard with his friend close to where his stepfather was working, remarked, "I'm going to see my dad tonight." When the play-mate remarked in a surprised voice, "But I thought that was your dad!" pointing to the stepfather, the youngster replied in a rather cool manner, "No, I mean I'm going to see my ex-dad!"*

Dynamics

The Stepfamily System

Before looking more directly at some of the concerns, it is important to understand the dynamics of the stepfamily system. There is never one system in any familiar group of relationships, but the number of possible relationships and interactions available in a stepfamily is sometimes hard to believe. In a biological family with two children there are six possible interactions or dyads. In this family of four were to split and one parent with the children were to marry again to a parent with two children, the minimum number of possible interactions or dyads would increase to 28. As in any system, there is a combination of subsystems that continue to exist, overlap and intertwine. Each must be considered. On the following Figure 1 are only a few, without going into any detail about the possible expanded number of relationships which in-clude the extended families of grandparents, aunts, uncles or cous-ins. The diagram of a relatively simple example will provide a better understanding.

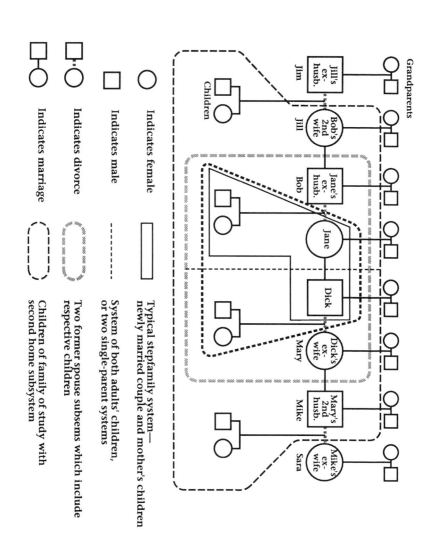

Figure 1. Stepfamily System

Oscar C. Christensen, Ed.D.

1. **The Divorced Spouse's Subsystem.** They are possibly still held together by a commitment to the children, by years of common history, by common friends, in some cases by genuine concern for each other, or by residual revenge and/or anger. The more years the first marriages were intact, the more difficult it is for people to disengage. If there is ongoing contact, as is usually the case when there are children involved, many of the old patterns of relating may continue. These once established patterns continue the stresses and tensions between the ex-spouses (or co-parents) and are usually carried into the present relationship.

2. **The Single-Parent Subsystems.** These include adults in the remarriage and their respective children. They can be particularly strong systems if there have been many years since the end of the previous marriage(s). The stress and anxiety that these single-parent families went through during the divorce and early stages of being alone can bring parents and children close together based on their mutual interdependency.

3. **The Children with Their Out-of-Home System.** This includes the other biological parent in a single-parent system or another stepfamily system. The children may move back and forth, either regularly or occasionally, but always within residual tension from one to another.

4. **The Biological Sibling Subsystems.** The alliances may be particularly strong as they have come through crisis together. As in the single-parent subsystem, these alliances may be held together because one parent may be perceived as having abandoned them for another adult. If the children believe they can break up this marriage (many times out of the mistaken belief that Mom and Dad would then get back together), they may work together to create extreme tension in the remarriage.

5. **The Step-Sibling Subsystem.** These are relatively new and quite uncomfortable at first, many times because of the unreasonable demands placed on them to act "like a family." As the two family constellations attempt to integrate into one system, stress and tension may be observed. If the age differences in the group are quite different, the competition may be less. If one group does not live under the same roof, the competition may only be strong when the two subsystems are merged. But if there is a blending of children, close in age, there will usually be rivalry and competition for a particular place of significance. Dreikurs says, "It is found that each child has an essentially different position in the family and must see all the circumstances of his childhood in an entirely different light" (1953, p. 37).

The first child in each system will be struggling to retain that special view of the world. The same is true, especially for the youngest child in both families, or any particularly significant role, such as only boy, only girl, the shy one, the athlete, the musician, etc. If the children are relatively young when this merging takes place (preschool age), the merger may be quite simple and accepted relatively quickly. Once a strong identity and significant place have been established by the children (usually elementary through high school), that merger may be overwhelmed by competition.

6. **The New Couple Subsystem.** The most fragile of all! These two people are struggling with their children, their identity as single persons, their prior claims (ex-spouses, in-laws) and yet at the same time, are attempting to do something that people in their early 20s are "supposed" to be doing—coupling. The knowledge that they may not have succeeded in this life task makes this marriage particularly significant. Dreikurs (1953) calls the life task of love the "most intimate union with someone of the other sex and represents the strongest and closest emotional relationship which can exist between two human beings" (p. 101). That process of coupling with everything that it entails, from romantic dinners to long talks about their future, takes on quite a different flavor when a number of children are always present.

It is hard enough to make the necessary accommodations while overcoming the fears of marrying again, but the additional factor of parenting, and particularly parenting somebody else's children, is almost overwhelming. The couple often will do anything possible to avoid arguments or any acts seen as destructive to the coupling. Therefore, the couple may find themselves "timidly and anxiously estranged, living through their days with suppressed yearnings and muffled screams, exchanging the contentious and exhausting pressure of their inner lives for an uneasy peace" (Napier, 1978, p. 147).

These six subsystems do not include ongoing alliances and relationships with grandparents, aunts, uncles or cousins, let alone the introduction of new grandparents, aunts, uncles or cousins, let alone the introduction of new grandparents, and others from the stepparent side. These alliances within and among the systems need to be understood and valued, both by stepfamily members and by counselors.

Characteristics of Stepfamilies

The work of Emily and John Visher (1979) is the basis for this discussion, as we have found no strictly Adlerian references to stepfamilies.

With possibly a little more of an understanding of what the systems look like, we can begin to focus on the dynamics in stepfamilies.

1. **A stepfamily is a family born of loss.** All members of this system have lost relationships, dreams, expectations, and/or life goals. Whether through divorce or death, no one in this relationship comes in without some degree of loss. In our society, most young people grow up with a certain set of expectations and beliefs about their adult life. There is a clear "ideal" way to marry and raise a family. When one realizes that a decision has been made either to divorce, to remarry or to marry someone with children, those previous expectations have been shattered. Many people rush into remarriage because they find it too painful to go through the grieving and loss of the first marriage. It seems easier to attempt to transfer all the positives from one relationship to another. However, usually the negative aspects of that relationship and each person's private logic come back to haunt them in the remarriage, but this time with an additional burden—the fear of failing twice!

   Children in stepfamilies have also experienced a major loss in their lives, some having adjusted and properly mourned—and obviously some not. Even for those that have come through the end of the nuclear family, the view of the stepfamily is one of loss—not gain—as the parents may have expected. They may now have to grieve the loss of a special role in the single-parent home, such as the incredible role of "head of household" or a special functional or emotional caretaker of the single parent. One stepparent who grew up with a stepfather said, "Having for eight years been the 'man of the house' and then feeling displaced by another man, I simply retreated into my room and didn't have much to do with this new family." Children will surely have to grieve the loss of the parent's time, special inter-dependencies, and that certain closeness established during the single-parent phase.

2. **All individuals in the family have previous histories.** There are traditions and values which exist that have nothing to do with this relationship and many times get in the way of "starting over." Each member brings into this relationship a portion of personal life style, which Dreikurs describes as the "ways and means which appear to be serviceable for his special plan" (1953, p. 53). Most young singles, coming into first marriages, have not had a sufficient length of time to develop traditions useful to them as an adult. They may have difficulties in their marriages as a result of incomplete separation from their family of origin. Remarriages may have difficulties because of incomplete separation from the previous marriage. As these traditions, values, and life styles merge, there may be major differences in events such as birthdays and holidays, but also in the subtle events of everyday life such as role assignments, language, and personal needs.

3. **The parent-child bonds predate the couple bond.** The single-parent systems have gone through crises together and usually have built strong boundaries against the outside world. To introduce a foreign element at this point is much like introducing a foreign element into a physical body—it will be rejected if at all possible. The parent of this previously single-parent family is also likely to participate in the subtle rejection of the new spouse, at the same time expressing excitement for the new relationship. Too much togetherness of the parent and child, too much siding for "my children," too much parenting of the children without involving the new partner, will result in the stepparent feeling rejected, isolated and outside the system. The single-parent subsystem can go on for a long time after the remarriage if the family does not integrate properly.

4. **There is a biological parent elsewhere with power and influence, even following the death of that parent.** "We have no set of beliefs, no language, and no rules for a family form that has more than two parents" (Furstenberg, 1980, p. 1). The stepfamily boundaries are ambiguous and constantly changing. They do not exist within the confines of a single home, but extend outside that home. The accepted pattern of one person in the role of father, and one in the role of mother, has to be redefined to understand that some aspects of the father's role may be assumed by the stepfather, while some aspects of the role of mother may be assumed by the stepmother. When children are living in the same home as a stepfather, much of the physical maintenance may be assumed by him, while the child may still receive much love and caring from the biological father. There are many combinations

of these shared roles, but they must be worked out to everyone's understanding and acceptance. If the out-of-home parent is unwilling to give up any of that role, the child will be caught in the middle.

Whether the children maintain two separate places of residence, only occasionally visit the out-of-home parent, or have virtually no contact, there is an emotional attachment that can be maintained for many purposes. There may be direct and constant ongoing contact and influence or more subtle influences maintained by the children or parents. Children may use this influence to insure that there is still love, or that there is always some place they can go if things get too rough. Subtle messages about that other parent can be used to manipulate or actually pull apart the new stepfamily.

5. **If the children have contact with both biological parents, they are, at least for periods of time, members of two households.** Even though we believe the ongoing contact with both parents is extremely important, this movement from place to place may increase the insecurity and instability for children. A deep sense of disloyalty may arise when the child makes statements of preference between households and/or parents. As children begin to feel comfortable and genuinely cared for by a stepparent, the loyalty issues again may arise as one begins to feel guilty about the positive feelings toward the stepparent. Many times competition between households is rampant as each parent tries to outdo the other as the "best" parent. Usually the children are caught in the middle. These issues lead to constant "culture shock" and a need for transition time as the child moves from home to home.

6. **There is no legal relationship between stepparents and stepchildren and their relationship will usually end if the marriage ends.** Without some kind of notarized authority, the stepparent cannot sign for medical emergencies, register children for school, or even sign up children for extracurricular activities. Knowing this makes it very easy for the stepparent to take a back seat in the responsibility for the family. It also makes it easy for the biological parent and children to accept that lack of initiative as a lack of caring or desire to be a part of the system. Anything that is seen as unimportant and temporary usually remains that way and the stepparent may never really integrate into the system. About a week before we were to be married, our four-year-old boy was playing his usual teasing game with Frank, laughing and having a great time. One of his ways to start the game is to express,

"I don't like you," usually with a big smile on his face. This time, Frank asked when he would start to like him, and with a rather surprised look he stated, "Well, when you and Mom get married, of course!" So even at that age, there were certain things that were left for a "real" family—obviously without the knowledge that his relationship with Frank could end just that easily, too.

Counseling

Counselor's Personal Issues

Before moving into the tasks or goals and process of counseling, certain personal issues must be faced when attempting to work with stepfamilies. Listed below are a few that should be considered and taken seriously before one begins this work.

1. Counselors need to be aware of their own values and beliefs concerning divorce, living together arrangements, and remarriage, and the possible impact of these events on the lives of children. One way to determine these would be to ask yourself these pertinent questions:

   a. Do you believe in and use the term "broken home?" This is a term and a belief that is viewed very negatively and with great suspicion by many divorced persons and stepfamilies. Most people who have divorced have felt the pain and agony of the home breaking while in their first marriage—and might leave a home before the actual separation occurred. However, after living through that agony, learning new life styles, new living skills and new ways of relating as a single-parent family and/or subsequently in a stepfamily, most feel that their home is no longer broken. They view their life style as one they have chosen and one in which they are working very hard to make it as positive as possible. They do not want to carry around the stigma of living a "broken" life forever.

   b. Do you believe children are always better off when there are male and female adults present in the home? Even though most divorced persons have lost one of their dreams of making a nuclear family work, they do not want to be confronted with a belief that their life is wrong or that it won't work or it will permanently "damage" their children. They do need help in believing that they can put their life back together again in a positive and productive manner beneficial for all members concerned.

c. Do you believe divorce or remarriage is a major factor in child behavior and emotional problems? There are two important aspects to remember: First, if one is expected to be "dysfunctional" (because of place in life, race, heritage, etc.) the result is often a very dysfunctional person. Secondly, there is little to suggest any correlation between intact dysfunctional families and behavior or emotional problems.

d. Do you believe stepfamilies should be able to function like biological families? Does your language or behavior imply that biological families are better than or stronger than stepfamilies? This is one of the major myths of stepfamilies and to believe it as counselors is a great disservice to clients. Stepfamilies cannot function like biological families, they never will and never should. But one of the major stresses the families face is attempting to "make" them into the mold of biological families without understanding the stress that results when this is tried. As counselors, one major goal is to help stepfamilies understand that they cannot be biological families, but that they can be as functional, as rewarding and as positive. No one can instantly love or instantly relate to another human being. All these human emotions take time and struggle.

If you have answered "yes" to any one of these, it may mean that more understanding of stepfamilies and their potential is necessary. This is not an attempt to define who should or should not work with stepfamilies, but rather to help counselors be better aware of how their values may hinder their counseling.

2. Counselors must learn the dynamics and understand the complexities of stepfamilies. As stated previously, counselors are encouraged not to accept the myths that these individuals can instantly love each other or recreate a biological family system.

3. Counselors need not allow the entire focus of counseling to be guided to the misbehavior of the "problem child." Adler contends that human beings cannot be studied in isolation (Adler, 1929).

4. The key element in a functional stepfamily is the couple. However, many times the partners deny their problems, which will be felt eventually and reacted to by one or more of the children. Clifford Sager says, "The therapist sensing that certain material is forbidden, may join the denial and thereby encourage the scapegoating" (1981, p. 2).

5. Counselors need to be able to tolerate ambiguity and chaos as they model patience and understanding of the process that needs to take place while the new family system becomes integrated. Sager says, "the therapist may attempt to allay anxiety by becoming over-controlling or by taking impulsive action. The therapist may rush too soon to try to impose order and consequently push the family away" (1981, p. 2).

6. As in all Adlerian counseling, the role of the counselor is an educator, model, and facilitator (Mosak, 1979). Additional actions that may be appropriate with particular stepfamilies would be to:

   a. provide ongoing support;

   b. listen and allow ventilation of feelings;

   c actively help to restructure and reframe situations;

   d. suggest active ways to achieve their tasks;

   e. facilitate the necessary bonding of the couple;

   f. remain a supportive outsider without being caught in the unrealistic expectations, myths, or feelings of helplessness;

   g. remain in control and be directive in interrupting and stopping interactions that are unproductive; and

   h. remain neutral without favoring one spouse, one child, or one ex-spouse.

Stepfamily Tasks as They Relate to Counseling Goals

There are a number of tasks that a stepfamily needs to accomplish before it can have a sense of wholeness and integration. These tasks, first enunciated by John and Emily Visher (1980), can also be viewed as goals for counseling. They are not developmentally in order, as they should begin immediately and continue throughout counseling and the life of the family. They will not be included under the process section because they may be important in different degrees and at different times with each family seen. If a family attempts to become a stepfamily without to some degree fulfilling these tasks, they may be overcome with difficulties. It is our assumption that stepfamilies which have been together and are finding life difficult probably have not completed these tasks successfully.

The *first* task is for all family members to mourn their own personal losses. The time and place of this mourning will differ for everyone. Usually children will delay and deny the loss of a parent for a great deal of time. They may continue to believe that somehow the parents will magically get back together. Remarriage may remove that final veil, forcing them to accept the previous loss of the other parent. All of a sudden life changes—Mom is expressing her affection to someone else, the parent has less time for the child, and the child may perceive the loss of a special place of significance in the family structure.

In the mourning process, the actual object is lost and must be mourned. However, the difficult loss to accept is the part of an individual, the personal role or significant place, that also has been lost.

Adults also must have mourned both their previous spouse and their loss of role in that relationship. If that has not been done adequately, the residual baggage from the former marriage too easily gets mixed in with the present one. The divorce rate for those who marry again within one year after divorce is almost double the average divorce rate of second marriages, again illustrating that it takes time and struggle to move through life's transitions.

With each of the tasks discussed we have included specific suggestions for intervention. For the first task:

a. Teach and model open expression of feelings, hopes and wishes to relieve the possible past reluctance or denial of grief. With children this can be done through telling stories, drawing pictures or writing letters.

b. Encourage acceptance and respect of each person to have the right to any and all feelings. Acting on feelings is quite different from having feelings.

c. Encourage movement through the grief process so that no one begins to use mourning for attention, power, revenge, or as disability.

d. Help explore anger directed to any person—it may be a stage of grieving rather than a personal attack.

The *second* task is the establishment and negotiation of new traditions and rituals. These include the obvious—such as holidays, birthdays, and vacations. But it also includes the not so obvious—such as language patterns, favorite words, ways of expressing affection, humor, decision making and conflict styles, role adjustments, and the ongoing everyday activities of the home. While expressing some of the fears, one remarried person who wishes to remain anonymous said:

> *I was so determined to make this marriage work, for the sake of myself as well as the children, that I would do anything to avoid conflict. For months after we were married, my new husband would get up early (which I could never understand, because my former husband had to be drug out of bed), read the newspaper, and when my alarm went off, immediately appear by my bedside with coffee, ready to talk and share his daily agenda. It took me two months to get up the nerve to share that I hated mornings, that it takes me at least $1/2$ hour to be alive, and that the last thing I wanted in the morning was a bright shining face eager to talk about the day. It was only when I couldn't stand it any more that I suggested he wait a half hour after my alarm went off to come in.*

Because it takes at least one year to have lived through all the holidays, vacations, and birthdays, and at least one more year to hint at being traditional, we believe in most cases a minimum of two years is required for the establishment of these traditions. This two-year time period is adequate for those families who realize ahead of time what the concerns, differences, and values are and are willing to negotiate and plan ahead. For the majority of families, however, the first few years may go by with little negotiation and a lot of resentment over such issues as who cleans toilets and when Christmas presents are to be opened. When people come into this marriage believing their way is the right way, negotiations break down before ever having begun, with resentment and misunderstanding being the norm. For Task No. 2:

a. Teach and model negotiation and decision making skills.

b. Encourage use of the family council or family meeting to plan ahead and negotiate requests and expectations.

c. Encourage open communication and respect so all persons have a right to say and feel for themselves.

d. Work with as much of the system as possible (including ex-spouses, grandparents, or any significant other) to work out details concerning the welfare of the children. Encourage the adults to make the major decisions, especially for small children, rather than forcing the children to choose between parents.

The *third* task of the family is the formation of new alliances while continuing to maintain the old. It is particularly important for children to feel that they have a right to continue their feelings for both parents while beginning to share feelings and interests with the new stepparent. This task relates back to the system and subsystem section. As the possible number of interactions, alliances and coalitions increases, there are innumerable possibilities for new relationships. If the biological parents and remarried parents encourage these new interactions, the children will not be faced with the ugly feelings of disloyalty to one, or guilt about caring for another. If, on the other hand, the new couple relationship is threatened by prior claims or there is ongoing animosity between ex-spouses, the children learn quickly that they are supposed to take sides—usually against their will.

One little boy who felt completely open in discussing his out-of-home parent in his new stepfamily exclaimed, "Why doesn't Dad and Mom get married again, and Jane (stepmom) and Bob (stepdad) get married, then we could all live together?" Even though the adults might see that as a horrendous idea, in his mind, the little one had solved his problem of wanting to be with all these people, but at the same time putting into perspective what he believed "should" be. For Task No. 3:

a. Encourage and actively work with the new couple to build strong, intimate ties by spending time together, exploring goals and a shared meaning for their relationship.

b. See the different combinations of dyads at different times, and encourage the dyads to spend time together. (Example: stepfather with each stepchild, stepmother with child, biological parent with biological child, etc.). Too many times there are always groups of people instead of one-on-one contact.

c. Suggest that the biological parent spend time away from the system on a regular basis—for meetings, shopping, so that the stepparent has full rights and responsibilities. This is often done if the biological parent is the father, but is less likely if the biological parent is the mother. Fathers, both step and biological, should be encouraged to interact with the children on a regular basis, apart from mom.

d. Very early in the work, establish what each person wants to be called, how they want to be introduced and talked about. (Examples: "This is my dad's wife," or "This is my stepmom," "Call me Lynn," or "Call me Mom," "I don't want to call you dad, I'd rather call you Frank, but I could call you Pop.") Negotiate the differences so that the issue of names can be resolved to everyone's agreement .

The *fourth* task is the integration and restructuring of this new family form. Part of this is the result of task number two, which is the manner in which life is lived. However, this task goes beyond that to a belief that this family form has value, can be successful, and is worth the commitment needed from every member. This family must be structured differently, with permeable boundaries for the give and take from people on the outside. This change in belief will partly influence society's beliefs about stepfamilies. But in a reciprocal manner, as society puts a higher value on this family form, new stepfamilies won't have the difficulties they now face. Society has always viewed a stepfamily as less than real, not good enough, an orphan of "real" families. If this value changes, so will individual families change to accept themselves. Possible interventions for Task No. 4:

a. Educate and help all members understand the complexities and confusions of stepfamilies.

b. Assess the stepfamily, and help them assess themselves, according to stepfamily norms—not biological family norms.

c. Encourage each person to express expectations of the relationship and help them explore the unrealistic myths.

d. Teach negotiation and conflict management skills so that planning and movement within and outside the boundaries can be done with less chaos.

The *fifth* task is centered more on the individual member of the household but also relates to the previous task. Each member of the stepfamily must begin a process of individuation and autonomy apart from, but within, the ambiguous boundaries of this family. Biological families might be able to function with dogmatic, autocratic structures. They may even function in a permissive home, but stepfamilies do not function well under either of these parenting styles. A stepparent cannot come into a home demanding, ruling, and controlling without the tradition, bonding, or trust established. On the other hand, if a stepparent comes in allowing anything to happen, the lack of attachment and respect will only prevent future commitment to the family or to the stepparent.

Oscar C. Christensen, Ed.D.

It is our belief that the only functional system possible in a stepfamily is a democratic system as described by Dreikurs and Soltz (1964), which allows equality among all its members and encourages respect for each person's worth. This includes the encouragement of sharing; the communication of opinions, thoughts, beliefs, and actions; the setting of legitimate limits with logical and/or natural consequences; and the belief in the worth of each person as a valuable, significant human being. It is in this kind of environment that members will begin the process of autonomy or individuation while at the same time learning the necessary skills of decision making, conflict management, communication, and respect for others. In this rather complicated system of ambiguous boundaries, undefined structure, countless relationships, and confusing feelings, the democratic system is the only possible workable structure. Possible intervention for Task No. 5:

a. Educate and model the principles of democratic families including: respect, natural and logical consequences, encouragement, responsibility for self, necessary skills, and family council (Dreikurs & Soltz, 1964).

b. Encourage in each residence (if children have more than one) a special place set aside for each child. Children need to feel that they belong. It could be a room, or just a special drawer to keep personal things.

c. Encourage the use of language which suggests stability, such as "living" in two homes (even if only occasionally) rather than "visiting" in one.

d. At an age-appropriate time, help adults to begin to back away from making arrangements, settling disputes, or requesting favors. Suggest and teach the children to begin to take responsibility for resolving these issues. This can be as early (for most concerns) as elementary school.

These tasks have been presented as a reference for a stepfamily's growth as well as a counselor's progress during counseling. In the following case study, many of these activities and goals will be illustrated in detail.

The Counseling Process: A Case Study

Ann: My daughter is having all sorts of problems and the school recommended that we see a counselor and they suggested you since you work with stepfamilies. The initial telephone call set forth the distress of a mother about her eleven-year-old daughter. She described the behavior—the daughter's grades had fallen; she had withdrawn from contact with her peers; she daydreamed a great deal and wasn't attentive in the classroom; and she had sudden outbursts of temper toward her sister and brother.

Counselor: I can understand your concern and we'd be happy to see you. What I would like to do is have the whole family come to see us.

Ann: Why everyone? It is Karin that's the problem.

Counselor: We feel very strongly that we need to begin with the whole family. Often when one child exhibits certain behaviors we would like to have the whole family work on helping to change that.

Ann (the mother), Michael (the stepfather), Karin, Kristin, and Kris Foreman came for the beginning of several months of counseling the following week. We knew they were a stepfamily of three years and that they were suddenly having a problem with Karin. With this little bit of information we began the counseling process, keeping in mind the many concerns of counseling stepfamilies.

First, we believe that it is important to focus on the family and not just the identified behavior "problem child." It is the family which is in conflict. Since this family may not only include the immediate step system, but also the original biological family system, counseling may include others, such as the ex-spouses, grandparents, and other important persons involved in the system.

Second, there are specific differences in stepfamilies of early formation and those that are more established. Young stepfamilies often exhibit conflicts over roles and positions and simply do not know what to do. Those families which come after several years exhibit entrenched chronic patterns that were not dealt with in the formative years. Research indicates that most stepfamilies coming for counseling are of the latter kind. Early formative stepfamilies, afraid of showing any sign of weakness or problems, usually stay away until they are in deep crisis.

Oscar C. Christensen, Ed.D.

Third, we recognize that stepfamilies come from different positions of need. Many simply want permission to share feelings, find new boundaries and establish their family. Some want information about stepfamilies and stepparenting. Others want to look at and work on options for their families. All of these are concerns for counseling, but are not necessarily counseling issues We expect most stepfamilies can be assisted to their satisfaction by centering on the first three concerns, though often couples and individuals may need to work on some deeper issues involving counseling.

Fourth, we will gather in the initial sessions some very basic data about the family. A "Stepfamily Checklist" (Visher & Visher, 1980) is helpful in constructing a base gathering data. These include:

1. How long has the stepfamily been together?
2. How long have the adult(s) lived in a single parent unit?
3. What is the relationship between stepparent and stepchild?
4. What is the situation with the ex-spouse(s)?
5. Are there money issues?
6. What is the relationship between the children and their other biological parents?
7. What changes took place for family members at the time of the remarriage?
8. Is there unfinished business with the former marriage?
9. What do the children call their stepparent?
10. Who makes the rules for the family?
11. Who enforces the rules in the family?
12. Who disciplines whom?
13. Are there sexual issues between stepsiblings or between stepparent and stepchild?
14. Are there difficulties after a child has been with the other biological parent?
15. How are holidays and special occasions handled?
16. Is the couple nurturing their bond?
17. Did the family start out in its own home?
18. What expectations are there for "love" and instant adjustment?
19. Where are the strong lines of loyalty?

We use many of the same techniques with both step and nuclear families, but always with an awareness of the complexities and unique stepfamily characteristics and concerns. The counseling has a beginning phase in which counselor and family get to know one another and data are gathered, a middle phase in which most of the real work is done by those families, and a termination phase. This corresponds to the Christensen-Marchant process in which their opening phase and data gathering concludes with a diagnostic hypothesis. The middle phase is a time of work with the family in changing behavior, giving information and redirecting goals.

When the Foremans came on the first evening, there was the normal amount of chaos that is present in any initial session. All five members of the family came and we initially sought to get to know one another.

We used some of the basic questions on the checklist, such as how long has the stepfamily been together? What are the ages of the children? What do the children call their stepparent? How long was the couple in a single parent situation? The answers give us an initial picture of the family.

Counselor: Why do you think you are here?

Kristin: (age 8) Because Karin has some problems.

Counselor: Why do you think the rest of you came?

Kristin: So we can help Karin.

Counselor: Would you also agree that it is also to help all of you—the whole family?

Kristin: I suppose so.

Counselor: I think that is probably why everyone is here. The family may have a problem and everyone is here to work on it. Tell me what your family is like: what you think is best about it and some things you'd like to change.

The family members proceeded to tell about their family. There had been a great deal of fighting among siblings and between Ann and Michael. The children expressed many resentments about one another and had a difficult time responding to the question "What is good about your family?" They had all kinds of suggestions as to changes they would like, including, "I want my mommy and daddy to get married again. Then everything would be okay." and "I don't like Michael" (stepdad). It was obvious from the beginning that the stepfather was on the defensive and feeling outside. Several times he sought to turn the discussion back to Karin. "We've got to do something about Karin. We're really worried about her." While acknowledging Michael's concern, we told them we needed to know more about the family.

Time was spent then on gathering relevant data about the which can be seen in the following genogram:

We discussed some of the roles in the family.

Counselor: Kris, when you fall down and hurt yourself, who do you go to?

Kris: (age 6) To Mom.

Counselor: And if she's not home?

Kris: Once in a while Karin helps me.

Counselor: And Karin, who do you go to if you are feeling bad?

Karin: To Mom, or I just go to my room.

Counselor: Karin, you help Kris and Kristin sometimes. Do they help you?

Karin: We help each other.

Discipline, one of the major issues, was also discussed briefly and it became clear that Ann did most of the disciplining and when Michael tried, the children would go to Ann for help or Ann would immediately intervene. Having found out some family information, we turned to the problem of Karin.

Counselor: Karin, it seems everyone is concerned about you. Do you want to talk about it?

Karin: I'm okay and I keep telling everyone nothing is wrong. It's the family that has problems.

Counselor: You feel that your family has problems?

Karin: Everyone's got something wrong more than I do. Everything's okay with me.

Counselor: You feel okay, but your school counselor tells us your grades have fallen and you daydream.

Karin: Yeah, I daydream sometimes.

Counselor: What do you daydream about?

Karin: About the divorce.

Counselor: Would you tell us about it?

Karin:	Well, Mommy and Daddy used to fight all the time and Daddy would slam the doors and walk out and Mommy used to throw things and they'd argue about us kids and who'd get us if they got a divorce. I used to put my pillow over my head so I didn't have to hear.
Counselor:	You feel very upset about their divorce.
Karin:	Yes.
Counselor:	Is that one of the reasons you're so upset in school and with your friends?
Karin:	They tease me all of the time. They tell me I don't have a real father and I tell them I do and fight them.

In further discussion we learned that Ann and Philip, her ex-spouse, had been separated nearly four years and divorced three. The children had first lived with her and then for a time, while she was out-of-state looking for work, with him; and now were back with her. Ann and Michael were married shortly after the divorce was final, but they had separated once during that time when she left the state.

It seemed important for the family to deal with Karin's issues immediately in order to lessen some of the family chaos. We realized that Karin had some very definite feelings about the divorce, her mother, stepfather, father, and herself. We asked if she'd be willing to write us a letter in which she'd be able to tell us anything she wanted to. It was suggested she might write a little bit each day and mail it so we'd get the letter before our next appointment. She readily agreed and the family seemed to relax with the knowledge that something was being done with Karin. With this issue handled, the session concluded, after an arrangement to meet with only the children the following week.

It was clear that although we didn't have all the data, some issues had already emerged, and we developed what Christensen and Marchant have referred to as a diagnostic hypothesis: (1) There was a strong alliance among the children, even with their fighting. (2) There was a strong alliance between the mother and children, illustrating the strength of the initial single-parent system. (3) There was a possibility of the daughter being pulled into a triangle between mother and stepfather, which became even more apparent in subsequent sessions. (4) The stepfather was an outsider trying to establish himself in the system with very little support from anyone. (5) There were clear role and rule ambiguities. No one knew

Oscar C. Christensen, Ed.D.

what one was supposed to do and to whom. (6) There were unresolved issues around the divorce and the mourning of losses was incomplete. (7) The communication patterns included very little listening or sending of clear messages. (8) The family constellation and discussion of roles suggested that Karin had the burden of being another parent.

The Vishers (1980) have set forth a series of issues to look for in evaluating initial data which we found helpful in looking at the Foreman family. These include:

1. Individual self-worth.
2. Who is left out?
3. Extent of couple unity.
4. What dysfunctional triangles exist?
5. Alliances and coalitions.
6. The existence of "boundary" problems.
7. The losses sustained by various members.
8. Areas of satisfaction.
9. Powerful figures outside the particular household.
10. What support systems exist—for whom?
11. Where the greatest resistance to change appears.
12. Acuteness vs. chronicity of the family situation.
13. Personal need for order and control and lack of ambiguity.

These issues helped us in making the initial hypothesis and in clarifying what additional information would be helpful in working with the family.

The second session was with the children. All of them came, eager to participate. Karin's letters, received before the appointment, revealed her despondency, anger, hurt, and thoughts of suicide. However, upon arrival, Ann and Michael indicated it had been Karin's best week in months and Karin indicated she felt much better and was getting along better with her peers. While there were other issues that arose later between Karin and Michael, it was as if Karin (and subtly the whole system) had accomplished her purpose: getting the family to do something about their problems. In fact, she had few other behavioral problems through the rest of the time they saw us.

Counselor: (to the children) How did you feel about the divorce?

Kristin: Kris wants to be with our daddy. He doesn't want to live with Mommy and Michael.

Counselor: Kristin, what do you want? How do you feel about everything that has happened?

Kristin: I don't like Michael. He yells at me and he makes Mommy cry sometimes.

Counselor: It sounds like the divorce has been hard on all of you—that you're still really upset by everything.

Having initiated the conversation about the divorce, the children were able to explore some of their feelings of loss. We found out that they were told by Ann that they weren't supposed to cry about it and that Michael was "here to stay" and they might as well accept it. Ann was seen in a very special place for all of the children. They had formed a very powerful single-parent system after the divorce and both children and mother were very protective of each other. This alliance left Michael feeling isolated at every turn.

Counselor: I'd like you to draw a picture of your family for me. Let's use the blackboard. Kris, why don't you go first?

The children drew a picture of their family, changed it as we talked about it, added to it, and explored its meaning. It became even more clear to us that the single-parent boundaries were still very closed. Ann was the center; Karin was nearest to her, then Kristin, and a I little further away toward the father was Kris. Kris stood on a line drawn to separate the children and Ann from their father and his girlfriend. Michael was 'way off to the other side separated by another line.

Figure 2. Foreman Family Drawing

Counselor: Michael is way over here. Why is he there when he's a part of your family now?

Kristin: Because we don't like him.

Counselor: So you might be wanting to get rid of him. How might everyone feel if you got rid of him?

Karin: We don't want to get rid of him. We just want him to be nicer. Mommy would be upset if Michael left.

At this point we explored what they remembered of the coming together of this new family. To the children, Michael suddenly appeared with little warning. They felt no one had told them about this possibility. We learned later from Ann that this was partly true. She and Michael had dated only two months when he moved into the house because he'd lost his job and didn't have any money. In the discussion with the children another issue arose.

Kris: Anyway, Michael caused Mommy and Daddy to get a divorce.

Karin: Oh, Kris, that's not true. Mommy told us that Daddy just made that up.

Kristin: He did not make it up. Michael took Mommy away.

This was clarified by Ann at the third session, when we learned that Philip was a very angry ex-spouse, believing that Ann and Michael had an affair and that it was this relationship that had broken up the marriage. He continually hinted at this to the children. According to Ann, she and Michael had not met until two months after the initial separation and did not begin to date for six months.

In the session with the children, Kris and Kristin's anger and their attempts to get rid of Michael were discussed. Karin was protecting both Mom and Michael. As we talked, it became clear that the children wanted a family that didn't fight, and if that happened Michael could stay.

We worked on the logical consequences (Dreikurs & Soltz, 1964) of their fighting and the children agreed to stop fighting and each of them would ask for special time with Michael. It became clear that while they didn't like the way things were, they also had not liked the fighting between Ann and Philip, their father. They also accepted that Michael was a part of their present family and that they needed to learn how to get along with him.

During this second appointment, while gathering more data about the family, the role confusion, the loyalty issues, the need for mourning, the ambiguous boundaries, and the "ghost of father past" became clear, and some immediate clarification of these issues was needed in order for this family to survive. We then scheduled an appointment with Ann and Michael in order for them and us to better understand the relationship between their previous marriages and their relationship with each other.

Ann: Everything is going so much better with Karin, except she and Michael got into an argument over when she was to come home from school.

Counselor: I'm glad that you're encouraged about Karin. Michael, how did you resolve the argument with her?

Michael: She won't listen to me. That's usually the way it is. She argued with me and then went to her mother and they decided what would happen. I just don't think I have a place with the kids. Every time I do something and Ann doesn't like it, she sides with the kids. If I don't do anything, she gets upset because I'm not involved.

Counselor: Michael felt like an outsider and this position was being encouraged by the strong parent-child subsystem. There was significant ambiguity in the roles, resulting in confusion for Michael and Ann as well as the children, over rules and discipline.

Ann: I don't like what he does when he disciplines the children.

Counselor: Would you be willing to tell Michael what you would like to have happen?

Ann: I don't want you to hit the kids and to listen to what they want before you say no.

Michael: It wouldn't matter because you'd still get in the middle.

It was decided that Ann would not interfere when Michael and the children had arguments and that they would talk through the problems with one another before making a decision, letting the children know that the decisions would be made jointly. This agreement between Ann and Michael relieved obvious frustrations between them.

Oscar C. Christensen, Ed.D.

Counselor: I'd like to move on so that we might better be able to understand your family. I hear a lot of the tensions and frustrations center around the children. What about the two of you? What is happening in your relationship?

Ann and Michael expressed concern because they felt things weren't going very well between them. They were arguing a great deal about finances, past relationships, and the children. Michael felt that the children were always the most important and he was at best fourth in line for any concern, affection or conversation. Ann felt that Michael didn't understand her role with her children. We pointed out to them the importance of the couple to the stepfamily that we believed that their resolution of the conflicts in their relationship was most important to the well being of the family. In this discussion we also gathered data about their previous marriages and their families of origin.

Michael had been married for six years. He and his ex-spouse had not seen one another since the divorce, nor had he seen his five-year-old daughter since that time, nearly four years earlier. He felt that his ex-spouse had abandoned him and therefore he didn't want anything to do with any part of their marriage, including their daughter. He had grown up as an only child with a very strict, dominating father and a weak, passive mother who took care of both males in the household. He related that he received no encouragement from his father, though he believed his father was a fair man and they enjoyed a good relationship. He didn't respect his mother because she "gave in so easily" and took emotional and physical abuse from his father. His first marriage to an "aggressive, dominant career woman" was filled with arguments and fights, ending with a great deal of bitterness.

Ann had been married for nine years. She and her ex-spouse were in contact with one another over issues pertaining to the children, but were arguing constantly over issues related to them—visitation, child support, values, rules, and their roles as co-parents. She felt that he was constantly interfering, but took no responsibilities. Philip saw the children only when he wanted to, usually after the children called him and asked to see him. He continued to blame Michael for the divorce.

Ann had grown up with one sister (four years younger), her mother, and "several men"—some stepfathers and some who just "lived in." Her father had left when she was five and she had not seen him since. Her mother had not formed lasting relationships with men and was a problem drinker. Ann left home at 12 to live with grandparents, returned to live with her mother at 14, and was married at 16. Ann didn't like her mother and had very little to do with her. She and her sister were very close and had gone through their childhood "protecting one another."

We realized that both Michael and Ann had many unresolved personal issues, mostly from the obvious anger which both carried about their family of origin. Their relationship was very fragile. They spent very little time with one another, were not in agreement about disciplining the children, and had a list of "garbage" each was carrying about their past relationships. Because of our belief that the key relationship in stepfamilies is the couple, we felt at this time that we needed to concentrate on them. It was evident that Michael did not want to be like his father, but had chosen a very critical wife. Ann had seen her mother use many men and she was now generalizing her anger to all men. This often came out at Michael, who was passive in their relationship but reacted out of anger by constantly changing jobs and remaining unemployed for long periods of time.

In our discussion with them we looked at the various family relationships—the strength of the single-parent system, the relationship of Karin and Ann, the weakness of the bond between Michael and the children, the ghost of Ann's ex-spouse who was very much a part of the family system, the sister of Philip, who with her three children lived with Philip's mother and who wanted Ann's children to live with her "for the children's sake," and the strong sibling system which was surviving through all of the turmoil. We encouraged Ann and Michael to begin to stop depending upon Karin to be the buffer between them, to be surrogate parent to the other children, and to be Ann's confidante. Ann and Michael agreed that Karin was in the middle much of the time and that they would begin working together instead of through Karin. We encouraged Michael to deal directly with Karin and not go through Ann for solutions to their difficulties. Michael agreed to spend one-on-one time with Karin and the other children. They both agreed that once a week Ann would leave Michael with the children.

Oscar C. Christensen, Ed.D.

Following the meeting with Ann and Michael we felt we had enough data to begin the middle phase of counseling. The next two appointments were with the whole stepfamily. At this time we tried to get the ex-spouse to come to a session with Ann and Michael and also sought to bring in Philip's sister. Both of them refused to come. The sessions included several issues previously discussed: (1) negotiating solutions to problems between Michael and Karin; (2) negotiating solutions to problems among Michael, Kristin, and Kris; (3) negotiating new rules and roles for everyone, including encouraging Ann to disengage from arguments; (4) talking openly about Philip and what the children wanted from the relationship with their father; (5) sharing of the relationship between Karin and Ann and, using pictures, letting them experience how triangles develop with Michael, Philip, and the other children; 6) discussing how conflicts between the subsystems get interrupted and never solved, such as Ann interrupting conflicts between Michael and Karin, or Karin interrupting the conflicts between Ann and Michael. The emphasis on negotiation is particularly appropriate from an Adlerian, democratic model (Dreikurs & Soltz, 1964).

In these sessions we used the stepsystem genogram to help the family understand the complexity of their lives, including the various relationships and the loyalties within the subsystems. This discussion helped adults and children in understanding the confusion and chaos in the family.

Between sessions Karin and Michael negotiated new rules with which both were happy and Ann remained outside their negotiating. Michael also began to spend more time with each child alone. Later Ann admitted that she was jealous of how well they were managing and realized that she was afraid of Michael becoming too close to the children. She feared the loss of her special place with them—a place she never had in her family of origin, in her first marriage, or in her relationship with Michael.

During the session with the family together, it became more evident to us that Ann and Michael were having a great many difficulties in their relationship. We raised the possibility with the whole family of spending several sessions with them alone. They agreed to see us in order to strengthen the couple bond and work out some of their difficulties. During these weeks we kept in touch with the children by a telephone call and by letters which they wrote. The family situation had eased for the time and it was the couple system that needed attention.

We continued to see this family for three more months. Ann and Michael each spent time working on residual issues from their first marriages and from their families of origin. In our sessions with the family together we spent much of the time encouraging what they were doing and giving permission for them to continue their struggle. The couple work that Ann and Michael did was effective in lessening many of their anxieties and giving them a sense of identity separate from the children. They were able to negotiate new boundaries for their life together around money, sex, work, and housework that had not been handled before. They developed an informal but written contract that spelled out their agreements.

The termination phase of counseling is often times difficult both for the counselors and the family. We had enjoyed working with this stepfamily. There were things we had wanted to do—work with the ex-spouse and other members of the wider system—which did not occur, but the experience for us had been positive. The children had responded to the experience and had grown from it. Ann and Michael had begun trusting and were looking forward to a future together. Several sessions before terminating we discussed ending counseling and what that meant. In the last sessions we shared additional resources available to the family. Ann and Michael joined a stepfamily support group, which was meeting regularly as a part of the program of the Stepfamily Association of America's local chapter. The whole family attended this group's activities, which put them in touch with other stepfamilies. We provided them with a bibliography and we left open the door to return in the future whenever they needed.

Not all counseling ends as positively as it did with the Foremans. They were willing to continue through the counseling to a jointly agreed upon termination. Many families, either feeling that they have everything under control and don't need anything more, or who get frightened by the experiences, simply stop coming. They have excuses for staying away and don't really terminate the counseling experience. Some families don't work through their problems and the result is often another divorce, as happens with 45 percent of second marriages.

We have, in this case study, attempted to show a process which takes into consideration the goals and techniques discussed earlier, providing an experiential process to go with the didactic.

Oscar C. Christensen, Ed.D.

Counseling the Stepfamily: Summary

In reading this chapter it is obvious that there are many similarities and differences in working with biological and stepfamilies. We've outlined below just a few of the most obvious. The similarities noted here can be compared to Christensen and Marchant's chapter as they describe Adlerian family counseling.

Similarities

1. There is a belief in democratic parenting and beginning immediately to model and educate about how to maintain a democratic environment.

2. The family may be seen initially together so that interactions can be observed and all members have a chance to participate. Counseling may eventually lead to couple or individual therapy.

3. The importance of understanding the purpose of each member's behavior in attempting to reach one's own personal goals is emphasized.

4. The use of many similar techniques such as typical day, life style, encouragement, and early recollections, are appropriate when assessing or clarifying the conflicts.

5. Working with all possible related people (school, out-of-home parent, grandparent, etc.) in facilitating change through the encouragement process is.

Differences

1. We believe in much more in-depth history taking. This could be integrated into the Adlerian life style as a method of assessment. There is simply more history to take—most of it full of loss, change and ambiguity.

2. We feel an immediate need to help a family lessen some of the chaos that is presently bringing them to counseling. It may be a conflict between two family members, a child's behavior problem or overall ambiguity.

3. The norms of a stepfamily are very different from those of a biological family. Any assessment must be made appropriately. A child moving back and forth is a norm in a stepfamily; a child coming and going would not be, in a biological family. A child having to deal with more than two parents is a norm, and so forth.

4. Even though one child may be in crisis when counseling begins, the focus will quickly shift to the family as a whole, rather than focusing on the scapegoated child. Some initial work with the child may be appropriate, but too much emphasis continues to deny the source of the concern, which is the family organization and the new couple.

5. Early emphasis on mourning and moving through loss is essential.

6. The complexity of the structure demands a therapist's creativity in keeping people organized and at the same time perceiving the situation from each person's point of view.

In reading and working with the concerns and problems of stepfamilies, we may be left with a perception of families which could never be functional and healthy. There are, however, many aspects of the stepfamily experience that are positive. Our emphasis in counseling is to remember the potential and to guide our clients to that positive experience of feeling "encouraged, optimistic, confident, courageous, and secure" (Mosak, 1979, p. 81).

Children in stepfamilies have a wide range of resources from which to draw comfort, support, care, information and values. With the increase of stepfamilies, the society has again moved toward a form of extended family with the potential for the wider experience offered in the three or four generational extended families of the early twentieth century. Children have the potential to gain an added sense of autonomy that is not always easy to find in biological families. There is movement, ambiguity, and change built into the system that necessitates and invites autonomy and responsible action. In learning how to move through the necessary changes and adaptation, children and adults have the potential for learning communication, conflict management, decision making, and negotiation skills. Children have a chance in a remarriage to view adults who are caring, loving, and probably sexually active. These demonstrations of affection may be avoided or nonexistent for many children in biological families. The modeling of intimacy, which preadolescent and adolescent young people can see, can be invaluable for them later in life. One young man stated, "you learn that adults have their problems, too. It was a hard lesson to learn, because I thought that adults were supposed to know everything..., but they're just as ridiculous as kids."

The remarried couple has moved through a number of transition periods in which they have had to struggle with loss, fear, identity and failure. If they have satisfactorily moved through these crises, they have much to give each other and their families.

The stepfamily can be an exciting, challenging and dynamic family form. Hopefully as the numbers increase and our society learns to value stepfamilies, the step system will be a valid and valued childrearing and adult nuturing setting.

References

Adler, A. (1929). Position in family influences life style. *International Journal of Individual Psychology, 3*(3), 211-227.

Ahrons, C.R. (1980). Redefining the divorced family: A conceptual framework. *Social Work, 25*(6), 438.

Capaldi, F., & McCrae, B. (1979). *Stepfamilies: A cooperative responsibility.* New York: Viewpoints Vision.

Dreikurs, R. (1953). *Fundamentals of Adlerian psychology.* Chicago: Alfred Adler Institute.

Dreikurs, R. (1967). *Psychodynamics, psychotherapy, and counseling: Collected papers.* Chicago: Alfred Adler Institute.

Dreikurs, R., & Soltz, V. (1964). *Children: The challenge.* New York: Duell, Sloan & Pearce.

Einstein, E. (1982). *The stepfamily: Living, loving, and learning.* New York: MacMillan.

Furstenberg, F., Jr. (1979). Recycling the family: Perspectives for a neglected family form. *Marriage and Family Review, 2*(3),12-22.

Furstenberg, F., Jr. (1980). Reflections on remarriage. *Journal of Family Issues, 1*(4), 443-453.

Glick, P.C. (1980). Remarriage: Some recent changes and variations. *Journal of Family Issues, 1*(4), 455-478.

Helping youth and families of separation, divorce and remarriage: A program manual. (1980). U. S. Department of Health & Human services, Administration for Children, Youth and Families.

Mosak, H.H. (1979). Adlerian psychotherapy. In R.J. Corsini (Ed.), *Current psychotherapies.* Itasca, IL: Peacock.

Napier, G. (1978). *The family crucible.* New York: Harper & Row.

Nichols, W.C. (1980). Stepfamilies: A growing family therapy challenge. In L. Wolberg & M. Aronson (Eds.), *Group and family therapy.* New York: Brunner/Mazel., 335-344.

Roosevelt, R., & Lofas, J. (1976). *Living in step.* New York: Stein & Day.

Sager, C. (1981). Difficulties facing therapists working with remarried families. *Marriage and Divorce Today, 6*(25), 23.

Seger, C., et al. (1983). *Treating the remarried family.* New York: Brunner/Mazel.

Visher, E., & Visher, J. (1979). *Stepfamilies: A guide to working with stepparents and stepchildren.* New York: Brunner/Mazel.

Visher, E., & Visher, J. (1980). *Stepfamily workshop manual.* New York: Stepfamily Association of America.

Visher, E., & Visher, J. (1988). *Old loyalties, new ties: Therapeutic strategies with step families.* New York: Brunner/Mazel.

Visher, J. (1981). Let's keep step. *Stepfamily Bulletin, 1*(3), 12.

Wallerstein, J.S., & Kelly, J.B. (1980). *Surviving the break up.* New York: Basic Books.

Oscar C. Christensen, Ed.D.

Chapter 5

Adolescents and their Families in Counseling

by Raymond Lowe

By Way of a Repudiation

While the title is couched in current parlance and probably serves to direct the reader's attention to a particular area of concern, the writer, at the outset, denies the validity of the long-established notion of "adolescence." Beyond the belief that there is no scientific evidence to support its existence, the concept, as it has evolved, has actually become a deterrent to positive motivation on the part of youth and to positive attitudes toward youth on the part of adults. Many of the difficulties parents, teachers, and youth themselves are experiencing can be attributed, in part, to that which underlies, conceptually, the social invention, "adolescence." A number of writers have postulated a "natural development" or "developmental deficiency" theory designed to explain away unacceptable behavior on the part of, so-called, adolescents.

Hodgman (1982) noted that while the term adolescence may be found in a fifteenth century Oxford Dictionary, as a functioning concept, it could not be afforded until the present century; it is a modern luxury.

Sigmund Freud and G. Stanley Hall, as early as 1905, reported on their studies of puberty and adolescence. More recently adolescence has been discussed by such notables as Anna Freud–psychoanalytic theory, McCanellness–dream theory, and Margaret Mead–anthropological theory, to cite but a few.

Following a critical examination of these and other theorists' positions, Gallatin (1976, p. 41) wrote:

I find it remarkable that there are so many theorists that accept adolescent turmoil as an unassailable fact of life when there is so little evidence to support this view. More or less normal teenagers, it turns out, do not experience inner turmoil, do not hate their parents, do not stage wholesale rebellion against society.

As a result of considering whose behavior bothers whom, one might postulate that adolescence is a period of inner turmoil experienced by well-meaning parents as they confront frustration with their children's experimenting with newfound feelings of autonomy.

Kohler (1981) directed our attention to an interesting fact. In terms of the readiness of youth to take their place as constructive members of society, she wrote:

Some "primitive" societies are more advanced than we are. In Africa, for example, many tribes expect male children to leave home at 13 or 14 .The youth receives a plot of land on which he builds his own home and lays out his own garden in preparation for the time when he will marry and start a family.... In contrast, our culture puts young people on hold... they are forced to be passive and dependent, deprived of the chance to make a difference in the world (p. 426).

What did Adler have to say about adolescence? References are found in several publications. However, it appears that they were taken from a single chapter in his most important book, *What Life Should Mean to You* (1931). For purposes of this discussion, his remarks are highly appropriate.

For almost every child, adolescence means one thing above all else: he wants to prove he is no longer a child.... But if he feels he must prove it, naturally enough he will over-stress the point.... While the parents try to continue their supervision, the child makes still stronger efforts to avoid control. The more parents try to prove he is a child, the more he will fight to prove the opposite. Out of this struggle an antagonistic attitude develops and we then are provided with a typical picture of "adolescent negativism" (p. 182).

Adler did not suggest that adolescence is a natural or instinctual phenomenon or even a normal one. Rather he suggested that it is social invention and hence a learned process, wherein an older generation of adults seeks to manage the lives of a younger generation of adults.

Oscar C. Christensen, Ed.D.

From the author's point of view, *adolescence is a social institution created to harbor and indulge individuals who are no longer children and who are prevented from assuming a viable position in a highly prized sociopolitical, technical, and affluent society.* Like so many social institutions, it has been created by one group to influence, if not control, the lives of a more vulnerable group. Those in charge are convinced the institution was created in the best interest of those for whom it was invented. The managers of adolescence resist change, especially that change initiated by teenagers. When changes have been initiated by the managers, often they are for the worse. The maintenance of this social institution has done less for those it was intended for and more for those charged with its maintenance.

In this chapter adolescence is viewed as a creation of Western civilization, developed and perpetuated to the end that the advantages of affluence and technology may be enjoyed by an older adult majority. It is in the affluent and highly technological Western world that adolescence has been institutionalized to the point that today it is regarded as both natural and normal. In maintaining the institution, youth, or young adults, are deprived of opportunities to gain a sense of being worthwhile through social contributions to their families and the community. In being deprived, they seek to feel worthwhile through peer associations, engaging in behaviors which are distressing to older adults: indiscriminate sexual activity, teacher harassment, school non-attendance, excessive use of drugs and alcohol, self-destruction, and other behavior defined as "general irresponsibility."

In a poll conducted by the National Education Association, "nine teachers out of ten say student behavior interferes with their teaching" (1981, p. 10). In another survey, ninety percent of high school seniors polled were critical of the nation's basic institutions (Etzioni, 1978). Eighty-six percent of middle class America sampled said sexual permissiveness was undermining the nation's morals (*Newsweek*, 1969, p. 47). Between 1950 and 1975 the annual suicide rate of white youths increased 171% (HEW, 1977).

Pearl cited the seriousness in disenfranchising youth (1978):

Yet the most notable aspect of the current situation of youth is the magnitude of their crime and employment problems and the inappropriateness of schooling to the solution of either.... If youth are to be valued, they must be of society-participants, not recipients.... adolescence is a "psychosocial moratorium".... Young people need a sense of usefulness. If they can't be useful to society...., they (will) invent ways to be useful to each other (p. 18).

A sense of uselessness among youth has become more intense as the institutional period of adolescence has been extended. As adults crave the advantages of affluence and technology, youth are increasingly relegated to levels of impotence-socially, academically, psychologically, politically, economically, esthetically, musically, and spiritually. Adults, unable to engage youth as participants in the larger society, attempt to prolong childhood. In this process, little of significance in the life of young adults is expected. Discouragement, commingled with apathy and excitement, accompany alienation. Erikson (1968), in discussing the problems and sometimes tragedies of youth, wrote, "Many a late adolescent, if faced with continuing diffusion would rather be nobody or somebody bad... than not be quite somebody" (p. 132).

In an effort to relegate youth to adolescents, a social policy has evolved wherein concern for generating caretaker institutions command adult imaginations, energies, and time—juvenile departments, self-identify and support groups, halfway houses, quarter-way houses, as well as school retention, military service, rigorous outdoor programs, and the like. These arrangements apparently give greater promise or seem more manageable than arrangements wherein youth would be taken into partnership, with full participation in the sociopolitical economic activities of the community.

The writer then, not wanting to perpetuate the myth of adolescence and believing any concept of adolescence is a contradiction when viewed from an Adlerian perspective, disclaims any support thereof. In short, he believes concepts of adolescence as well as teenagers (1) have no basis in fact, (2) are inventions designed to cope with youth in an advanced technological society, (3) are substitutes for responsible participation, (4) are destructive of viable self-concepts, and, finally, (5) have no meaningful place in Adlerian thought.

Oscar C. Christensen, Ed.D.

Precursors and Theoretical Perspectives

The precursors to parent-youth counseling described herein are found in the Individual Psychology of Alfred Adler and Dreikurs' principles and techniques associated therewith. These are ably discussed elsewhere in this and other references. (Adler, 1923; Adler, 1930; Adler, 1963; Ansbacher, H. & R., 1956; Christensen, 1980; Corsini & Manaster, 1982; Dinkmeyer & Dreikurs, 1963; Dinkmeyer & McKay, 1976, 1980, 1983; Dinkmeyer, Pew, & Dinkmeyer, 1979; Dreikurs, 1968; Dreikurs, Corsini, Lowe, & Sonstegaard, 1959; Dreikurs & Grey, 1968; Lowe, 1982, 1983; Lowe & Morse, 1982; Sweeney, 1975; Terner & Pew, 1978).

These and other references explore the background, activities, theory, principles, and techniques generally associated with the Adlerian child guidance movement, more recently and probably inaccurately referred to as Adlerian family counseling. Among the more important concepts underlying the Adlerian child guidance movement, initiated in Vienna by Alfred Adler and systematized in America by Rudolf Dreikurs, are social interest, purposeful behavior, encouragement, family constellation, family atmosphere, goals of disturbing behavior, methods of training, recognition reflex, democracy, belonging, logical and natural consequences, mutual respect, inferiority feelings, inferiority complex, and autonomy, all discussed elsewhere in this text. The parent-youth counseling described herein has its roots in Adler's open child guidance centers. The counseling process, only recently developed, differs markedly in technique.

A review of Adlerian/Dreikursian literature reveals little information about counseling parents and youth together in an open setting, ,though several excellent references exist. Gould (1977) has presented a number of excellent ideas intended for parents seeking to improve their interactions with their youth. The reference has proven most helpful to youths. Walton also has succinctly articulated a number of critical concerns, procedures, and suggestions for parents, teachers, and counselors (1980).

Mosak and Mosak have compiled a comprehensive bibliography of Adlerian writings (1978). They indexed 35 publications focusing on adolescents, over 500 pertaining to children, and 58 centering on family counseling and child guidance. Those on family counseling appear to be limited to counseling focusing on parent-child problems. The literature on adolescent techniques relates, for the most part, to youth counseling with peers with but incidental involvement of parents.

The Current Predicament

The issues which call for new approaches to parent youth cooperation have emerged from radical, social, technological, economic, and political changes. Our heritage of autocratic forms of control, a heritage which for centuries stood the test of time, is without foundation today. To complicate matters further, the issues common to parent-child conflicts are quite unlike those concerns reported between parents and youth. Problems, far more prevalent among youth than children, involve separation, misuse of drugs, unemployment, dropping out of school, and destructive sexual activity, as well as the desire for independence and the refusal to cooperate with parental demands.

Efforts to improve the situation by parents and other adults often lead to greater conflict, frustration, and defeat. Parents, in their social and emotional bankruptcy, turn to legal resources only to find them wanting: understaffed and, in many instances, no better informed as to what to do than the parents themselves.

It is out of reflections on these and related matters that the author developed a counseling program for parents, teachers, and youth with the philosophy that each can profit from what the other has to offer, thereby gaining a sense of usefulness and significance. It is because youth are, in many instances, denied opportunities to gain their objectives that they turn to useless and destructive methods, with the mistaken belief that through them they will find a place of sustaining importance among their fellows.

A Distinction Between Counseling and Psychotherapy

Because of the confusion prevailing among professional practitioners as to the meaning of the terms, "counseling" and "psychotherapy," for purposes of this chapter, a distinction is made. While Dreikurs and others have made a distinction between "counseling" and "psychotherapy," this distinction is not shared by all Adlerians. Counseling, in general, and as it applies to Adlerian parent-youth counseling in particular, is best exemplified by Tyler (1960) in her notions of counseling for minimal change. Here the counselor functions less as a therapist and more as an educator facilitating understanding of the nature of the concerns, while suggesting options for parent-youth relationship change. Psychotherapy, on the other hand, is for those who profit little from awareness, as typified

Oscar C. Christensen, Ed.D.

by "I know what I ought to do but I just don't seem to be able to do it!" In such instances, greater skill and knowledge are required to assist clients in making basic changes in their personalities or life styles.

Purpose, Approach, and Assumptions Underlying the Center's Functioning

The purpose of the counseling venture is to encourage parents, teachers, and youths to work cooperatively and effectively in the many situations which bring them together. The approach to resolving parent-youth conflicts utilizes the group progress and the assessment of group dynamics. Parents, teachers, youths, and other interested persons, under the leadership of the counselor, consider the nature of the relationship, options for improving the relationship, and share in deciding the activities to pursue toward resolving the conflicts. These counseling sessions are open to professional and lay persons, at no charge.

The assumptions underlying the approach are a more controversial matter. Without scientific certainty as to why some people experience difficulty in their relationships and, further, lacking scientific assurance as to the most efficacious approach to helping these people, many in the counseling profession have settled for ill-formed assumptions as the basis for their practice. Parent-youth counseling described here is no exception.

Assumptions provide the basis for theory. They are often derived out of considered thought, repeated patterns of experiences, persistent study, and even flashes of insight. The assumptions of the author are taken from Adlerian theory, and integrated with ideas gleaned from twenty years as a parent-youth counselor. These assumptions include:

1. When the opportunity is realized, parents and youths prefer to live harmoniously.

2. Parents and youths in conflict will listen to and interact with a third party when they refuse to listen to or interact with each other.

3. Parents and youths in conflict express their thoughts and feelings more freely in an open counseling session, than in the privacy of an office.

4. Commitments by parents and youths made in an open session are more likely to be carried out than the same commitments made in the privacy of an office.

5. Many families observing open-center counseling have problems in common with families being counseled.

6. Observers of parent-youth counseling are encouraged to make changes in their lives as a result of the efforts and results, both positive and negative, accomplished by parents and youths being counseled.

7. Students and professional practitioners alike will validate their academic learning.

8. The process and techniques used in parent-youth counseling are validated immediately, as the session proceeds.

9. The community, in continuing support of the center, or the denial thereof, participates in ongoing evaluation of the efficacy of the counselor and the counseling process.

10. The center assists individuals in gaining a sense of belonging to an important effort as they participate actively or passively, in the process of changing parent-youth relationships.

The Counseling Setting

The setting for parent-youth counseling is somewhat similar to that characteristic of parent-child counseling. It may be conducted in one of a variety of locations: a school, church, university, community college, public lecture hall, theatre-in-the-round, public library-any place that will accommodate the many activities essential to the center's function. Primary to the decision as to the center's location are a number of considerations not the least of which include suitability of space, operating budget, convenience of access, use of the space by others, custodial services, circumstances of possible clients, size of audience, extent of need of audio assistance, and the political machinations associated with anything new to a community. Wherever the location, it must be one where people feel they want to be.

The center, directed by the writer, is cosponsored by a university and the local school district. There is no budget for the program nor are there any fees. The center is located in a junior high school noted for its unique approach to providing its youth an education. The counseling sessions take place in the cafeteria, one evening a week, for two hours. The clients and the co-counselors are seated at a table on a raised platform. The table is centered in the room with 250 chairs, arranged in concentric circles. Audio-video equipment includes four to six microphones, video cameras, a video tape recorder, amplifier, and four speakers equally dispersed behind the last row of chairs.

Oscar C. Christensen, Ed.D.

The gymnasium across the hall is used as a playroom for young children. Several classrooms are scheduled for parent study groups, youth study groups, playrooms when the gym is otherwise scheduled, and university student discussion groups. These activities are scheduled simultaneously with the parent-youth counseling sessions.

A receptionist's station is located close to the cafeteria entrance where information is provided about the scope and function of the center. Restrooms are in close proximity. The evening custodial staff provide assistance in performing several services essential to smooth functioning.

Provisions for refreshments provide modest amounts of money for playroom materials and snacks. Students and other observers who attend regularly assist in setting up and taking down chairs, bringing in a large portable blackboard and the portable platform, and cleaning up following the session.

Conditions for Receiving Counseling and Audience Participation

Any family where parents or youths are experiencing difficulty in their interpersonal relationships, regardless of the location of their residence, are afforded counseling services. While it does not happen frequently, sessions are held wherein teachers and youths are counseled for the same purpose.

Specific conditions for receiving counseling are (1) attending at least two, two-hour sessions as observers; (2) requesting an intake interview which is conducted, usually, in the family residence; (3) granting permission to confer with school and other agencies concerned for the youth's welfare; and, (4) participating in a parent or youth study group. These study groups enable parents and youths to discuss, in groups of eight or ten, the nature of their relationships and, further, some ideas for improving these relationships.

Staffing the Center

The extent of staffing is dependent upon the nature and scope of the services to be provided. Those essential to the center described herein require (1) a center coordinator; (2) an associate coordinator for administration; (3) an associate coordinator for staff and counselor training; (4) an intake interviewer; (5) a receptionist/ librarian; (6) parent or youth study group leaders; (7) a role-playing director; (8) a counselor who typically doubles as the coordinator; (9) co-counselors; (10) audio-video operators; (11) a recording secretary; (12) and a playroom director (Figure 1).

Counselor's Role and Function

The counselor's role is defined by the functions one performs. The counselor assists parents, teachers, and youths in learning techniques and principles to improve their relationships, and gaining an awareness of how they each contribute to their relationship problems. In addition, the counselor may provide supervision of co-counselors and act as a leader for the center staff, its clients, and the supporting public. To perform these tasks the counselor must be (1) well-informed about the socio-psychological dynamics of the culture in which the client functions; (2) highly skilled in interviewing multiple clients; (3) equally skilled in supervising counselor trainees; and, (4) a competent teacher for the larger group. These skills are exemplified through the appropriate use of interviewing, role playing, interpreting purposeful behavior, brief lectures, group discussion, and encouragement, all based upon Adlerian and Dreikursian practice, as well as adaptations by the author.

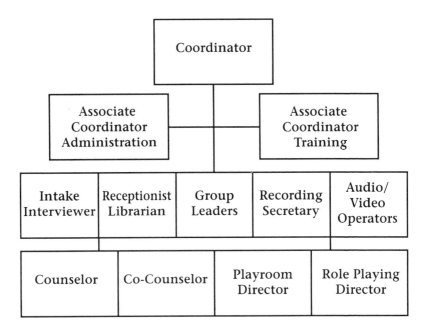

Figure 1.
The Community Parent-Youth Education Center Staff

Oscar C. Christensen, Ed.D.

The Flow Charts

Flow charts, as described by Christensen and Marchant, are provided to enable the reader to gain, in graphic form, a visual perspective of the counseling process. The charts, which follow, project the three principal components of the parent-youth counseling program: the preparation period prior to the counseling session (1.0), the counseling session (2.0), and the post-counseling session (3.0). Later, the subsystems will be cited and discussed (Figure 2).

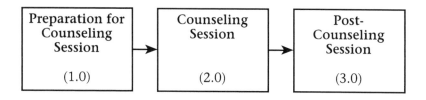

Figure 2.
The Principle Components of the
Parent-Youth Counseling Program

In this chapter, the flow charts are appropriate portrayals of what exactly takes place in a typical parent-youth counseling process. They are used to represent, generally, what is intended. They include what is considered essential to the counseling process and the likely temporal sequence in which situations are considered. The interactions, purposes, thoughts, principles, and techniques, of necessity, vary according to the mode of expression used by the clients and the ability of the counselor to integrate one's skills with the attitudes and information presented by each family member. The charts, then, are presented for clarification of the total process rather than prescriptions for it.

Preparation for Initial and Subsequent Interviews (1.0)

Weekly staff meetings are conducted just prior to the counseling session, usually the day before. At this time, the agenda for the staff session is directed toward activities to take place the following evening (Figure 3).

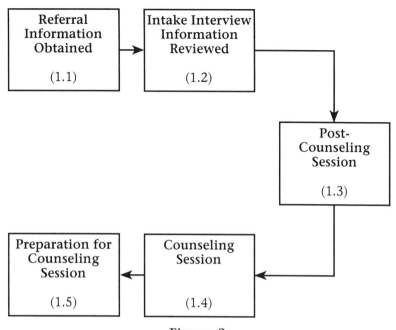

Figure 3.
Preparation for Initial and Subsequent Interviews

The preparation session starts with information gathering about the family to be interviewed for the first time. This begins with the intake interviewer identifying the family. It is the interviewer's task to gather and present all pertinent information. Names, ages, and other identifying items of family members are placed on a chalk board, for example:

The Jones Family

Grace, mother, 36, part-time secretary

Bob, father, 36, architect

Bob jr., male, 16

*Tamie, female, 14

Susie, female, 11

The asterisk identifies the individual of greatest concern to the parents. Often times, the parents are at a loss as to what to do about any of the children!

Details for the initial interview include who, why, and how a family came to be referred (1.1). Subjective situation data, who is complaining about whom, and the purpose of each family member attending, are presented and discussed. Additional information gathered from the family physician, school personnel, and other agency representatives interested or concerned about the situation, is also noted at this time (1.2).

The next phase in the preparation process is most important (1.3). At this time the coordinator conducts an exploratory discussion for the purpose of integrating this information into a tentative plan of action, as well as for the purpose of staff training. The plan of action reflects particular approaches, timing, and sequences which seem appropriate for counseling. Speculation as to what the objective parent-youth relationship might be, and how best to validate this speculation, is an essential part of staff training. A review of these hypotheses takes place at the staff meeting which follows the counseling session.

Normally, a second family joins the first family in the counseling process. The scheduling of families is such, that in any one session a new family is interviewed along with a family that has been interviewed previously. Thus, an initial interview and a follow-up interview are conducted during the same session. Data gathering for the family scheduled for a subsequent interview is less detailed than that for the initial session. The co-counselor assigned to the second family provides the information essential to the staff preparation meeting. Information gathering centers on any crisis which may have happened since the last session, and additional information from school or other agency personnel.

The fourth item on the agenda involves assigning the co-counselor to the new family, while identifying the co-counselor previously assigned to the second, or follow-up family. At this time, the counselor and co-counselors (counselors in training) outline the role they will take in the interview session (1.4).

Finally, brief reports as to unusual events, help needed, or protracted plans by other functionaries takes place: the group leaders, the playroom director, the role-playing director, the receptionist-librarian, the recording secretary, and the audio video operators (1.5).

It must now be apparent that for a center to function smoothly, the scope and function of each task must be clearly defined and specifically assigned. This is accomplished, in part, by a handbook in which these tasks are identified and role relationships delineated. The weekly staff meetings help to maintain the clarity of role relationships.

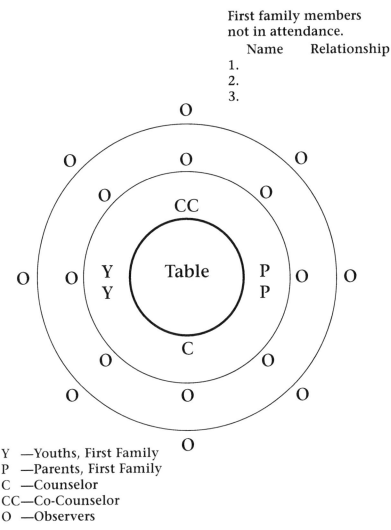

First family members
not in attendance.

	Name	Relationship
1.		
2.		
3.		

Y —Youths, First Family
P —Parents, First Family
C —Counselor
CC—Co-Counselor
O —Observers

Figure 4. Seating Arrangement for Initial Session

Oscar C. Christensen, Ed.D.

Initial and Subsequent Counseling Sessions (2.0)

While some description of the physical arrangements within the center has been provided, more specific details as the seating placement of the family members, the counselor, and the co-counselor are provided in this section. The counselor and the co-counselor are seated at a round table opposite each other, and the parents and youths are sitting beside the counselor and co-counselor opposite each (Figure 4).

A facsimile of the seating plan is drawn upon a chalkboard indicating the names of those seated at the table. Beside the facsimile are listed the names, ages of children and youths, and other identifying information of the family members not in attendance. This may include grandparents, other siblings, a parent not living in the family but with whom the children have frequent visits, and so on. The schema enables the observer/audience to follow the family drama as it unfolds and as names of "significant others" are introduced from time to time. It further serves as visual reminder of the family constellation. The sequence of the actual counseling session is summarized in Figure 5. Subsequently, additional detailed representations within each subcomponent are provided.

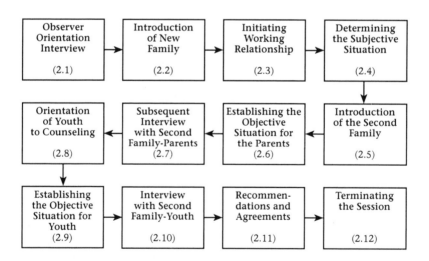

Figure 5. Sequence of Counseling Session

Observer Orientation to the Initial Interview (2.1)

The counselor begins the session with a few brief remarks, two to three minutes, addressed to those observing the interview (2.1.1, 2.1.2, 2.1.3). The counselor initially asks who is attending the center for the first time (2.1.1). This is followed by comments focusing on the purpose of the counseling process: to assist members of the family in improving interrelationships within the family (2.1.2). The orientation concludes with the counselor establishing certain ground rules for audience participation (2.1.3).

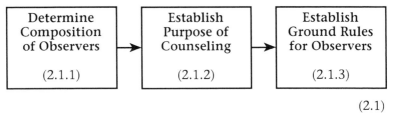

(2.1)

Figure 5.1.
Observer Orientation to Initial Interview

These ground rules include the following: all inquiries must be within the Adlerian/Dreikursian frame of reference and if this frame of reference is unfamiliar, the observer is asked to wait until a later time and seek clarification from any staff member; all inquiries are restricted to clarification about the counseling process; no inquiries directed at families being counseled will be entertained. It is essential that members of the audience not misconstrue clarification with argumentation. There often is someone in the audience who wants to "take the counselor on" in terms of philosophy, theory, ethics, or competence.

Introduction of the New Family to the Counseling Process (2.2)

The new family has some awareness of the counseling process, inasmuch as members have attended at least two sessions as observers and have participated in the intake interview. The intake interviewer has brought the family to the table and they sit as noted.

Following remarks to the observers, the counselor introduces the co-counselors and the family to the audience (2.2.1). Unless otherwise noted, this is the first time the family will have met the counselors.

　　　　　　　　　　　　　Oscar C. Christensen, Ed.D.

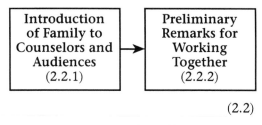

(2.2)

This arrangement is intentional. It allows each person attending to begin formulating one's thinking and learning at approximately the same time and place in the interview sequence. The counselor, being sensitive to the quality of the parent's and youth's relationship as they sit opposite each other, offers remarks appropriate to the task of establishing a relationship conducive to the counselor's and the family's working together (2.2.2).

Initiating Working Relationships (2.3)

While a constructive working relationship between the center staff and the family members hopefully begins at the first moment a staff person interacts with a family member, it is not until this point in the sequence that the counselor capitalizes on earlier staff contacts and begins establishing a constructive working relationship with the family i .

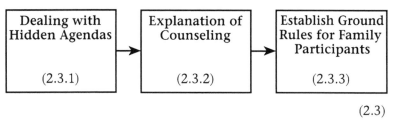

(2.3)

Figure 5.3.
Initiating Working Relationships

Normally, when a family comes for counseling, each family member is most certain as to one's virtues and positive attitudes, and well-rehearsed as to the vices and disturbing behaviors of the others. Each wants a hearing to establish these "facts" and in so doing seeks the understanding and support of the counselor. This is more common among parents than youth. It is because of this hidden agenda that it becomes incumbent upon the counselor to convey to each family member that the counselor has no interest in taking sides (2.3.1). Rather, the counselor's stated purposes are to (1) understand the dynamics of the relationship, (2) to interpret what purpose the relationship serves for each, (3) to consider alternatives to the current relationship, and, (4) to assist each in pursuing alternatives intended to improve the relationship. All efforts in any other direction should be considered carefully to determine whether or not they are counterproductive to the purposes for which counseling is offered (2.3.2).

The introductions cited earlier (2.2) begin the counseling relationship building process. At this time the counselor establishes the parameters within which the dialogue will take place by laying down the ground rules by which participants are expected to abide. Inasmuch as family members heard them and observed their application while in the audience, they hopefully come as no surprise (2.2.3). The rules for participation are simple. They include an agreement that when there is a face-to-face dialogue each will respect the other's right to complete statements without interruption. When there is a face-to-back seated position, the person behind will maintain silence until seating is reversed. In any event, acceptance of the counselor's decision as to when exceptions are warranted will prevail.

The Subjective Situation (2.4)

The subjective situation represents the views of parents and youth about their mutual conflicts. While the parents and youth are seated opposite each other (Figure 4), the counselor urges them to express their concerns about what is, or is not, going on. This phase in the process is referred to as the interaction experience (2.4.1).

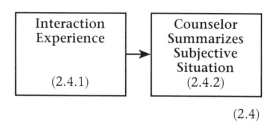

(2.4)

Figure 5.4. Determining the Subjective Situation

In a brief period of time, three to five minutes, the subjective situation is established. In instances where hostility between parents and a youth runs high, the audience frequently is shocked.

Daughter: (To father) I hate your guts; I can't wait until I'm old enough to get out of that hell hole.

Father: (To daughter) The feeling is mutual; the sooner you get out, the better.

It is the counselor's task to use one's knowledge of the Adlerian view of human motivation, coupling it with skills in negotiation and communication, while counseling with spontaneity, humor, and dispassion. As the interaction escalates:

Counselor: Is there any question in anyone's mind about what goes on in this family? What do we know that we didn't know before?

The counselor then proceeds to review how each member of the family thinks and feels, with some guesses as to the dynamics of each striving to find a special place within the family. Hypotheses as to why there might be disharmony among family members are appropriate at this time (2.4.2).

Having established the subjective situation, a reseating of the family takes place. The parents remain at the table while the youths are seated behind their parents. At the same time the second, or follow-up family is invited to join the group. The follow-up parents are seated opposite the first family and their youths behind them (Figure 6). The names and other identifying data of those at the table, as well as those not in attendance, are added on to the chalkboard. The co-counselor for the second family also joins the group at this time.

Introduction of the Second Family (2.5)

As the co-counselor is introduced, attention is given to the uniqueness of the second family members' participation (2.5). These citation, include (1) the important role they play in assisting the counselor in the counseling process; (2) their role in offering encouragement to the first family, based on their experience and learning; and, (3) their increased confidence in their abilities to participate constructively, as result of offering this encouragement. Some brief comments an usually offered by the counselor to bring the second family into the process and at the same time allude to their past concerns.

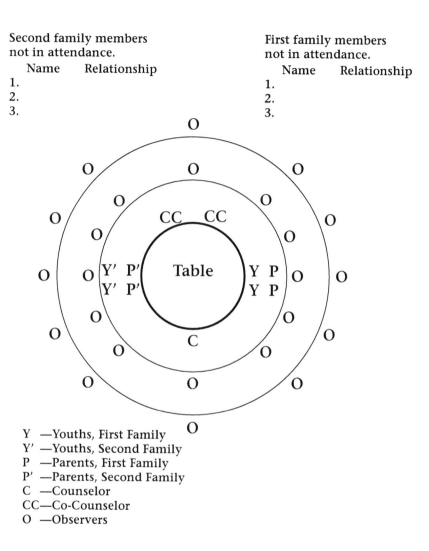

Second family members
not in attendance.

Name   Relationship
1.
2.
3.

First family members
not in attendance.

Name   Relationship
1.
2.
3.

Y —Youths, First Family
Y' —Youths, Second Family
P —Parents, First Family
P' —Parents, Second Family
C —Counselor
CC—Co-Counselor
O —Observers

Figure 6.
Seating Arrangement with the Second Family

Establishing the Objective Situation for the Parents (2.6)

The counselor, following the introduction of the second family, proceeds to interview the parents of the first family for the purpose of establishing the objective situation. For the Adlerian, this includes the following questions: What is the nature of each person's private logic? How does each person go about seeking to find a place in the family? Which consequences prevent their achieving a constructive role? At this point, the parents' mistaken approaches and private logic are explored and examined. Unlike the subjective situation where members of the family freely complain about what others are doing or not doing, the objective situation defines the problem in terms of purpose and consequences.

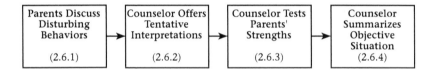

Figure 6.1.
Establishing the Objective Situation for the Parents

The counselor establishes the objective situation by soliciting specific examples of disturbing behavior from each parent. (2.6.1). For each example, specific instances are cited. Following the citing of a "for instance," the counselor probes to determine the interaction which took place between the parent and youth and, especially, how the parent felt about the interaction. It is at this point in the interview that the counselor is provided with a basis for validating earlier guesses as to the purpose of each individual's behavior.

Mother: I don't like it when Mary tells me she's going to a friend's home and later I learn she didn't go there at all. And worse than that, she had no intention of going there in the first place.

Counselor: When did this happen last?

Mother: Just last night!

Counselor: Tell us what happened.

Following an explanation the counselor speaks:

Counselor: And what did you do about it when she finally did come home?

Mother: I did what any mother would do. I chewed her out! I told her she was heading for the same kind of life as her sister.

Counselor: And how did you feel about it all?

Mother: I felt pissed! I can't trust her anymore!

Clearly we have here a confrontation of power. The mother requires, the daughter does what she pleases; the mother insists, the daughter ignores orders.

The counselor continues with questions and offers interpretations and possible options. These might include: "What would happen if you were to...?" or "What is the worst thing that could happen if you didn't...?" This phase of the interview session is intended to test the parents' strengths (2.6.3). What are the parents willing to do differently? Are they interested in resolution or conquest? Do they understand, if not appreciate, that the youth may be trying to make a point about what they believe to be an impossible situation? The parents of the second family are also urged to raise questions or offer suggestions from their experiences since they began their counseling sessions. The co-counselor may participate in much the same manner.

This part in the interview sequence may require twenty or twenty-five minutes. A brief summary of what seems to be taking place is offered by the counselor with assurance that at the end of the session, following a discussion with the youth, specific homework in the form of recommendations will be assigned (2.6.4).

Subsequent Interview with Second Family Parents (2.7)

It is now time to discuss the concerns, efforts, successes, and failures of the second family. With the first family remaining at the table, and after a few words intended to move the focus from the first to the second family, the counselor typically inquires:

Counselor: Well, how are things going with the Rhoades family?

Mr. Rhoades: Well, some things good; some things not so good.

Counselor: Good! Will you remind us what you were going to work on?

Oscar C. Christensen, Ed.D.

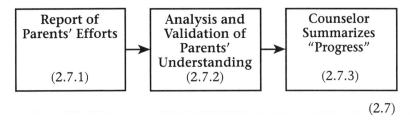

| Report of Parents' Efforts (2.7.1) | → | Analysis and Validation of Parents' Understanding (2.7.2) | → | Counselor Summarizes "Progress" (2.7.3) |

(2.7)

Figure 6.2.
Subsequent Interview with the Second Family

As with the first family, a subjective report is made of the parents' ideas as to what took place in carrying out the homework. The reports range from enthusiasm to discouragement (2.7.1). Whether they are reported as positive or negative experiences, each incident is analyzed. Sometimes parents will report an experience as positive when, upon analysis, it was discovered that they didn't understand the recommendation and superficially "improved" the situation. More often parents will report their experiences negatively. Frequently, upon analysis, it becomes clear that much of a constructive nature actually took place. This phase is identified as the validation of parents' understanding phase (2.7.2). The report and analysis requires fifteen or twenty minutes. Finally, the counselor tentatively summarizes an assessment of the relationship and justification—consistent with Adler's ideas about struggling to find their place in the group and the kinds of behaviors, often disturbing, in which people engage when they feel unsuccessful (2.7.3). This concludes the exploration of the parents' view of the problems, and the counselor's assessment of the parent-youth dynamics.

At this time the parents exchange seating positions with their youths (Figure 7). The importance of this exchange is noted in subsequent sections of this chapter.

The challenges confronting the counselor are different from those facing youths and their parents. The counselor has completed an interview with parents, who, generally speaking, are, in the presence of the counselor and the audience, more or less acquiescent. They have come eager to learn what they hope will be effective ideas for the management of the lives of their children. The counselor can expect that since most parents have been frustrated in their past collective efforts, they do come to the session with what might be identified as a healthy skepticism toward the process. Typically, this is also the case with youth. "This is just another old fogey who is going to tell me to respect my parents or my teachers!" and "He's going to tell me he knows what's best for me!" characterizes the attitude of many youths during the first session.

Second family members
not in attendance.

    Name   Relationship
1.
2.
3.

First family members
not in attendance.

    Name   Relationship
1.
2.
3.

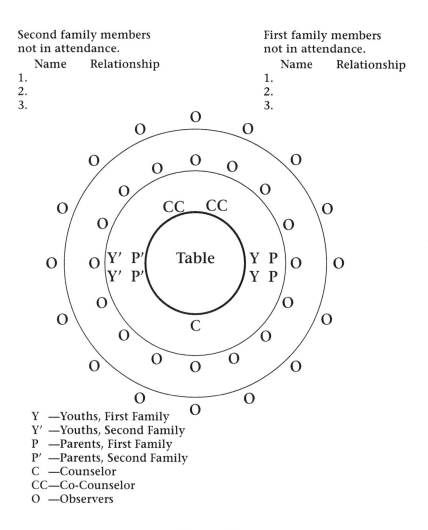

Y —Youths, First Family
Y' —Youths, Second Family
P —Parents, First Family
P' —Parents, Second Family
C —Counselor
CC—Co-Counselor
O —Observers

Figure 7.
Seating Arrangement After the Exchange of Seats

Orientation of Youth to Counseling (2.8)

It is obvious by now that a new set of challenges confront the counselor. How, in Dreikursian terms, do you "win" the youth?

One cannot influence anybody unless one has first established a friendly relationship.... If a good relationship exists, serious disturbances of cooperation hardly even arise.... There is only one element which all effective methods share: sincerity.... Children are able to size up any adult within a few seconds. If he tries to put up a front, the child immediately senses his pretense. Children respond to anyone who has the courage to be as he is with all the faults and shortcomings that human beings possess. (Dreikurs, 1968, p. 59)

Dreikurs was addressing these remarks to teachers, but they are equally applicable to the counselor relating to youth. The counselor must be extremely sensitive throughout the sessions, but particularly during the initial session, to preclude being labeled as "just another disappointed adult." How the counselor interacts with the youths' parents, the nature of the language used by the counselor, the emphasis placed on any particular behavior, and the position taken by the counselor toward the parents' or youths' concerns, do as much to persuade the youth as to whether or not the counselor has anything to offer (2.8.1).

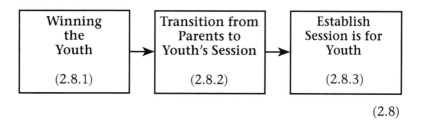

(2.8)

Figure 7.1. Orientation of Youth to Counseling

To move from emphasizing parents' concerns to those of youth, a few remarks are appropriate. They are designed both for purposes of transition as well as gaining the confidence of the youth (2.8.2).

Counselor: Thanks for being patient. It must have been hard a few times there when your folks seemed to be taking you apart. But as Fred (youth from the second family) knows, this is your session. As you didn't interrupt your parents, they know that they are not allowed to interrupt you. It may be harder for them than it was for you. They spend so much time correcting everybody! Did you notice how Mom corrected Dad when he said you brought the car home late Tuesday night when it was actually Wednesday night?

The youths are encouraged to speak freely (2.8.3). The counselor states to the audience:

Counselor: It is important that we not give justification to the youths' conviction that they are alienated. We are not here to find fault with what may or may not have been done. Youths take care of that pretty much in their own way, often times punishing themselves through guilt feelings.

Finally, as part of this orientation, the counselor notes the probability of their not agreeing with what the parents have said.

Establishing the Objective Situation for the Youth (2.9)

The subjective situation, as viewed by the parents and youth, was established at the outset (2.4. It is now time to establish the objective situation of the youths: What are they doing in their efforts to gain a sense of significance? How do they feel about the results of their efforts? How do they find their place in the group?

This phase of the session begins with the counselor seeking responses to the youths' view of the parent session (2.9.1).

Counselor: Well you've heard Mom and Dad, what do you think? Have they been fair?

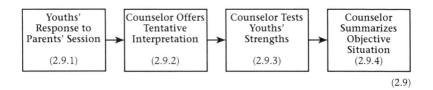

Youths' Response to Parents' Session (2.9.1) → Counselor Offers Tentative Interpretation (2.9.2) → Counselor Tests Youths' Strengths (2.9.3) → Counselor Summarizes Objective Situation (2.9.4)

(2.9)

Figure 7.2.
Establishing the Objective Situation for the Youth

Establishing the objective situation of the youth is similar to the approach followed with the parents (2.6). If there are two or more youths, the counselor listens to where there is agreement or disagreement among them. Where there is disagreement, the counselor probes for explanations, noting who blames who and how each handles the other's accusations. With each accusation, whether it be against the parents or each other, the counselor asks "And what do you do about it?" or "What do you want to do about it?" and "What keeps you from doing something about it?" Here, the counselor is seeking to establish responsibility, not for what the relationship is, but rather, for what each *wants* to do about it. Between complaints and accusations, the counselor seeks to provide understanding of both the parents' and the youth's behavior. A typical interaction between counselor and youth might be (2.9.2):

Counselor: Why do you think your parents came down so hard on you ?

Youth: I don't know. They're always on my case!

Counselor: Don't you have any idea?

Youth: Nope.

Counselor: May I tell what I think?

Youth: Yeah, I guess.

Counselor: Could it be that they don't know what else to do? They're so damned frustrated; nothing works. "We'll just give him hell?"

Youth: Maybe.

Counselor: You don't like them coming down so hard on you. I wouldn't like it either. What would you have them do when you don't follow through with what you said you would?

Youth: I don't know, I just want them off my case!

The counselor now has some indication as to the extent of the youth's pampering (Rattner, 1971). The next step is to determine the extent to which the youth wants to work on improving the relationship. At this time, the youth's strengths are explored and tested. What level of confidence does the youth possess? How much is one willing to compromise and give one's parents a chance to help? To what extent is the youth discouraged? What kind of encouragement is appropriate in seeking the youth's cooperation (2.9.3)?

In bringing this phase of the interview to a close, the counselor summarizes what the situation is and what is probably necessary for it to change (2.9.4).

Subsequent Interview with the Second Family-Youth (2.10)

It is now time to focus on the concerns and efforts of the youths of the second family (2.10.1). The counselor listens carefully, clarifies perceptions, and provides encouraging comments whether the reports tend to be positive or negative. It is particularly important for the counselor to identify positive gains, even though the youths spend much of the time complaining about their parents or each other.

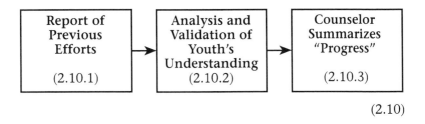

(2.10)

Figure 7.3.
Subsequent Interview with Second Family—Youth

The analysis undertaken by the counselor seeks to provide understanding where misunderstanding prevailed, an Adlerian interpretation where punitive misinterpretations were offered (2.10.2). Finally, the counselor summarizes what one believes to be the gains made with some exploration as to what possible next steps might be taken (2.1 0.3).

Recommendations and Agreements (2.11)

By this time the counselor has facilitated a discussion of parent-youth concerns, offered interpretations, directed parents and youth towards relationship change. It is now time to explore recommendations, sometimes called homework, to be undertaken between the session and the next one, usually occurring in two weeks (2.11.1). Often, parents are eager to work while youths are willing, sometimes reluctantly.

Oscar C. Christensen, Ed.D.

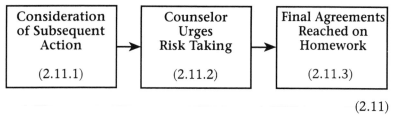

(2.11)

Figure 7.4. Recommendations and Agreements

The counselor, taking advantage of positive attitudes, urges a risk taking posture (2.11.2). Emphasis is placed upon what each is willing to do without regard for what the others agree to do. The fact that one might "blow it" is acknowledged as simply being human, that the individual might be encouraged to accept mistakes and not give in to self-defeat. In those instances where one of the others experiences a setback, each could make allowances and, whenever possible, support the transgressor. The counselor notes that there are three specific times when it is appropriate to attempt to improve a relationship: before the fact, during the fact, and after the fact. In any event, these efforts should be undertaken only when parties concerned are willing to listen and consider a different approach (2.11.2).

Now is the time to settle on the homework. The counselor asks each member of the family, "What do you want to work on between now and next time?" It is most important that all focus on what they can do to handle themselves before, or during, or after a conflict arises. It is equally important that each works on one concern at a time. Working on several tasks at a time affords excuses for doing nothing. In addition, the counselor obtains an agreement that each family member will do nothing to interfere with the others' efforts (2.11.3).

Terminating the Session (2.12)

At the conclusion of the session the counselor anticipates that there will be "yes, buts," and "what ifs" from any of the family members. It is not unusual, therefore, to find one sibling raising questions about another sibling:

Mother: Yes, but what if she doesn't come home when she agreed to?

John: (Sibling, referring to his brother.) What if he still takes my bike when he said he wouldn't?

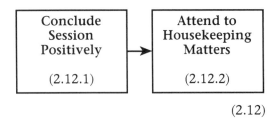

(2.12)

Figure 7.5. Terminating the Session

The neophyte counselor typically falls into the client's "trap" and proceeds to offer a host of ideas as to what might be done. Clients who raise such questions after agreements are reached are revealing their skepticism, discouragement, or reluctance to give up their desire to manage others. The counselor must be resolute in conveying, kindly but firmly, that the session has come to a close.

Counselor: Let's see what happens. If we were to consider all the possible ways something could go wrong, we could go on forever. We'll cross that bridge when we come to it, okay?

The counseling concludes on a positive note. The counselor might call attention to some dramatic change that has taken place, thank people for attending, offer to help any of the visitors, suggesting they speak to or leave their phone number with any member of the staff, and, in the spirit of cooperation and participation, ask all attending to help with the cleanup and other housekeeping matters (2.12.2).

As the center is being closed down, the counselor, co-counselors, and families retire to a corner of the cafeteria where an informal discussion often continues. A general inquiry such as, "How do you feel about what went on this evening?" is often made. Remarks intending to provide assurance for observers or family members are directed to the person(s) who appeared unusually upset. Counseling staff responses generally takes the form of, "I know it isn't going to be easy but we have to work on it." The family is reminded that while the staff doesn't want to encourage clients to become dependent, they may call the co-counselor.

Oscar C. Christensen, Ed.D.

Counseling Review Session (3.0)

Following the interview, the staff meets to review the counseling session and to make plans for what is to take place during the week, in preparation for the next session.

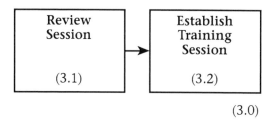

(3.0)

Figure 7.6. Counseling Review Session

The review focuses on questions about objectives, techniques, and theory which grew out of the session (3.1). Following this review a few minutes are required to schedule the training sessions for the co-counselors (when video tapes are reviewed) and the parent and youth study group leaders (3.2). Finally, the day and time for the weekly administrative session is confirmed. At these sessions, the coordinator, associate coordinators, receptionist, and the playroom and role-playing directors confer about administrative matters essential to a smoothly functioning center.

Some Thoughts While Shaving

No single approach to helping parents and youths has consistently demonstrated its superiority over any other approach. Current methods for determining relative efficacy are wanting. At the present time our beliefs are stronger than our knowledge. It is just possible that the human condition will never lend itself to a precise quantitative analysis. Our cultural variations in aspirations and values may render theoreticians and practitioners impotent in establishing a common ground for knowing the efficacy of family counseling. This dilemma confronts the parent-youth counselor who is seeking to validate counseling interventions.

The parent-youth counselor is probably most effective when integrating a frame of reference (Adlerian-Dreikursian, in this case) with the particular expectations of the parents and youths who are attending counseling. As somewhat of a scientist, counselors assess their own efficacy on the basis of observable change in their clients. These observations often lead to the conclusion that "I do what I do because it helps people change, and thus makes sense to me." Similarly, the procedures in this chapter should be adapted so they make sense to the reader, whether teacher, counselor, or psychotherapist.

References

Adler, A. (1923). *Individual psychology*. London: Routledge & Kegan Paul.

Adler A. (1930). *The education of children*. New York: Greenberg.

Adler, A. (1931). *What life should mean to you*. New York: Putnam.

Adler, A. (1963). *The problem child*. New York: Capricorn.

Ansbacher, H., & Ansbacher, R. (1956). *The individual psychology of Alfred Adler*. New York: Basic Books.

Christensen O.C., & Thomas, C.R. (1980). Dreikurs and the search for equality. In M.J. Fine, (Ed.), *Handbook on parent education*. New York: Academic Press.

Corsini, R.J., & Manester, G.J. (1982). *Individual psychology*. Itasca, IL: Peacock.

Dinkmeyer, D.C., & Dreikurs, R. (1963). *Encouraging children to learn: The encouragement process*. Englewood Cliff, NJ: Prentice-Hall.

Dinkmeyer, D.C. ,& McKay, G.D. (1976). *Systematic training for effective parenting (STEP)*. Circle Pines, MN: American Guidance Service.

Dinkmeyer, D.C., & McKay, G.D. (1980). *Systematic training for effective teaching (STET)*. Circle Pines, MN: American Guidance Service.

Dinkmeyer, D.C., & McKay, G.D. (1983). *Systematic training for effective parenting of teens (STEP/Teen)*. Circle Pines, MN: American Guidance Service.

Dinkmeyer, D.C., Pew, W.L., & Dinkmeyer, D.C., Jr. (1979). *Adlerian counseling and psychotherapy*. Monterey, CA: Brooks/Cole.

Dreikurs, R. (1968). *Psychology in the classroom.* New York: Harper & Row.

Dreikurs, R., Corsini, R., Lowe, R., & Sonstegard, M. (Eds.). (1959). *Adlerian family counseling.* Eugene, OR: University of Oregon Press.

Dreikurs, R., & Grey, L. (1968). *A new approach to discipline. Logical consequences.* New York: Hawthorn.

Erikson, E . (1968). *Identity and the life cycle.* New York: Norton.

Etzioni, A . (1978). The crisis of modernity: Deviation or demise? In A. Pearl, D. Grant, & E. Wank, (Eds.), *The value of youth.* Davis, CA: International Dialogue Press.

Gallatin, J. (1976). Theories of adolescence. In J.F. Adams, (Ed.), *Understanding adolescence: Current developments in adolescent psychology.* Boston: Allyn & Bacon.

Gould, S. (1977). *Teenagers: The continuing challenge.* New York: Hawthorn.

Hodgman, C.H. (1982). The kid that grows on you: The American adolescent today (and tomorrow). *Rochester Review,* Winter.

Kohler, M.C. (1981, February). Developing responsible youth through youth participation. *Phi Delta Kappan, 62,* 6.

Lowe, R.N. (1983). Adlerian/Dreikursian family counseling. In A.M. Horn & M.M. Ohlsen, (Eds.), *Family counseling and therapy.* Itasca, IL: Peacock.

Lowe, R.N., & Morse, C.L. (1982). Parent-child education centers. In C. Hatcher & B.S. Brooks, (Eds.), *Family counseling and therapy.* Itasca, IL: Peacock.

Mosak, H.H., & Mosak, B. (1978). *A bibliography for Adlerian psychology.* New York: John Wiley.

NEA Research. (1981). Disruptive behavior. *National Education Association,* Nov.-Dec.

Newsweek, October 6,1969.

Pearl A. (1978). Toward a general theory of valuing youth. In A. Pearl, D. Grant, & E. Wenk, (Eds.), *The value of youth.* Davis, CA: International Dialogue Press.

Rattner, L. (1971). The pampered life style. In A.G. Nikelly, (Ed.), *Techniques for behavior change.* Springfield, IL.

Sweeney, T.J. (1975). *Adlerian counseling.* Boston: Houghton Mifflin.

Terner, J., & Pew, W.L. (1978). *The courage to be imperfect.* New York: Hawthorn.

Tyler, L.E. (1960). Minimum change therapy. *Personnel and Guidance Journal,* 38.

U.S. Department of Health, Education, and Welfare; Public Health Service; National Center for Health Statistics. (1977).

Walton, F.X. (1980). *Winning teenagers over in home and school.* Columbia, SC: Adlerian Child Care Books.

Chapter 6

Marriage Counseling and Enrichment

by E Clair Hawes

Introduction

The marriage counselor is both a therapist and educator. When a couple comes for help with marital problems, the counselor helps them to see that their problems may be caused by a lack of information about the skills essential to living in an intimate relationship. The main role of the counselor is to facilitate the development of these skills. This role is fulfilled through a counseling process which elicits and integrates information which the couple already has about their relationship.

The purpose of this chapter is to articulate one model for the marriage counseling and enrichment process. Basic principles of Adlerian marriage counseling will be presented and exemplified through a flow chart and case examples. Throughout this chapter, the reader is encouraged to make personal modification of this model in order to improve his or her understanding and integrate already existing information about the marriage counseling process.

The Marriage Counselor's Role

There are several principles of Adlerian theory that help to define the role of the marriage counselor. One guiding principle is concerned with the changing societal view of marriage. Many forms of marriage and couple relationships abound today; the counselor must be aware of these and accepting of the type of marriage that a couple purport to want for themselves. Marriage counselors must clearly understand their own values so that they do not impose these on their clients or present a limited concept of what is possible within their relationship.

The Adlerian marriage counselor takes an optimistic view that most marital problems can be worked out as long as there is a relationship of mutual respect and cooperation (Dinkmeyer, Pew, & Dinkmeyer, 1979). This optimism helps the counselor to be an agent for change by fostering an environment where there is a sense of balance between each partner. The marriage counselor attempts to give each side a fair hearing to facilitate cooperation, while not being sidetracked from the basic Adlerian problem-solving question, "What's the situation?" and the subsequent, "What can we do about it?"

The financial reality of most counseling settings requires that the marriage counselor work alone. Therefore, the counselor must immediately elicit the confidence of both partners and establish a position as a trusted, objective third person who can mirror the ineffective dynamics of the relationship and teach more constructive methods of interaction. At the same time, the marriage counselor must point out the strengths that exist, and encourage their use as a firm foundation on which to mend or rebuild the marriage. As the couple's trust is gained, they allow the counselor to be a part of what, until now, has been a closed dyad. This privileged position is usually developed within the first interview, as the couple is being asked to share feelings and issues with the counselor that they may not have risked discussing honestly with one another.

It is essential that the couple perceive the marriage counselor as being emotionally stable. They depend on the counselor to have the strength and perspicacity to either support or protect the couple, individually or together. A case example is particularly illustrative. Tim is six feet, four inches tall and weighs 250 pounds; his wife, Janice, is five feet, two inches tall and weighs 110 pounds. Even though the marriage counselor is only slightly larger than Janice, Tim told the counselor:

> *"When Janice and I start discussing issues in your office I know I can go full out and say all the things I've been avoiding because I've been afraid I would steamroll right over her and do irreparable damage to either of us. I can rely on you to stop me, so I discover what I'm really thinking and feeling as I talk here, and it feels good because its safe."*

A final aspect of the marriage counselor's role is the need for flexibility. Many novice marriage counselors feel that they are confined to a process or particular technique that seems rigid and inflexible. Fortunately, most counselors find that as they practice their skills and monitor their own progress, concurrent marriage counseling sessions become more efficient and effective. Each counselor's unique style, as well as demonstrated care and concern, will soften or round out the techniques employed.

The Marriage Counseling Process

The marriage counseling process described in this chapter and attending flow chart is based on five structured, one and one-half hour weekly sessions, with an indefinite number of successive sessions. The material covered is unlikely to take less than five, but could easily extend to eight or more sessions. The variables depend on the intensity and number of presenting problems, whether or not a crisis currently exists which must be dealt with before the education and enrichment process begins, how articulate each partner is, and how quickly a rapport is established between the couple and the counselor. Both the couple's and the counselor's goals of counseling must be closely aligned; once this is established, it is possible to move from step to step on the flow chart (Figure 1).

The flow chart is not intended to lock each step into separate compartments; it is to establish the direction of each session and to ascertain that the counselor takes the responsibility for movement rather than getting mired in, for example, numerous accounts of the wrongdoings of each partner by the other. If an education process is going on, there must be an opportunity for the counselor to present ideas and alternatives to the couple.

In response to criticism that the flow chart is a cold, mechanical method for communicating a very warm, human interaction, the following analogy is offered:

A *sheet of music is a cold, inanimate object or model that contains only lines and musical notation This sheet of music can be used by a skillful musician to produce beautiful sounds for your enjoyment. One could, of course, play an instrument or sing in a very mechanical way. In fact musicians usually do perform in a mechanical fashion until they have received sufficient training and practice* (Stewart, Winborn, Johnson, Burks, & Engelkes, 1978, p. 31).

This chapter is structured to enable the reader to follow a case example through the five-session model. Each session description is described in terms of the flow chart functions, with a presentation of the counseling dialogue and accompanying commentary. Throughout this chapter the reader is encouraged to think of other interventions that might have been effective with this couple or others.

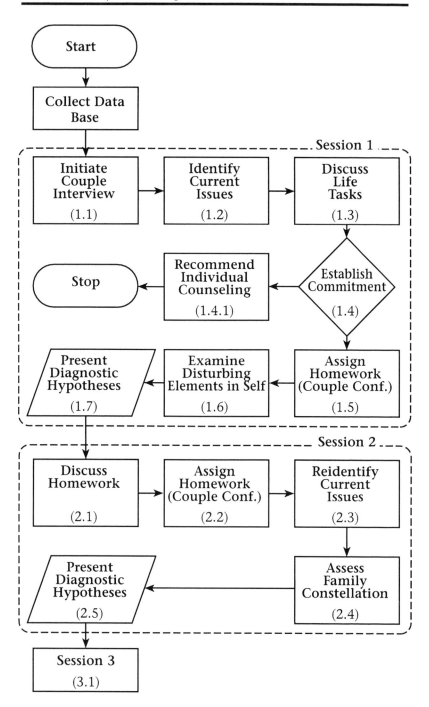

Oscar C. Christensen, Ed.D.

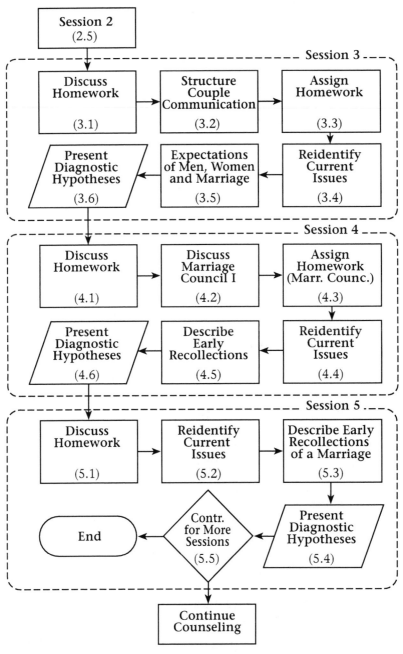

Figure 1.
Flow Chart of the Marriage Counseling Process

The Referral

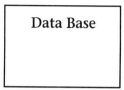

Data Base

When a couple first comes for counseling there is rarely a reliable data base (see Christensen and Marchant chapter). Referrals from other professionals often provide information based on a model wherein there is definitely something "wrong" with one or both partners, or that one of the partners is to blame. Such data is seldom an accurate reflection of what is going on in the marriage. If the couple has been referred by friends, value judgments have probably been made on the relationship as to who is at fault, and the couple comes with a burden of guilt. It is the first responsibility of the counselor to establish an atmosphere conveying the attitude "What is happening and what can we do about it?" rather than "Who did what to whom and why?" The counselor demonstrates mutual respect by accepting that each partner's presentation is that person's reality, even though each differs from the other's, and is very subjective data.

Very often marriage counseling is the outgrowth of individual therapy with one of the partners. As it develops from individual counseling that the marriage relationship is the basic concern, it is important that both partners attend counseling. The success of this transition often depends on how able the marriage counselor is in helping one partner to invite and encourage the participation of the other. If the absent partner refuses, it may become evident to the attending partner that the other has little intention of working to improve the relationship through counseling, and the client must be helped to deal with that reality as a separate issue. Marriage counseling cannot be done without the presence of both partners. To help one partner deal with the frustrations of the marriage as one perceives them without the presence of the other is not marriage counseling; it is individual counseling .

A reliable data base, then, generally involves little more than names, addresses, and telephone numbers. Other pertinent data will be collected informally during the life task section of the first interview.

Oscar C. Christensen, Ed.D.

Session One

```
Initiate Couple
Interview
(1.1)
```

When a couple arrives at the initial interview, the counselor must be aware of how uneasy they feel and how threatening an office may be. Many misconceptions prevail about what goes on in the marriage counselor's office based on dramatization in the popular media. A limited discussion of a social nature is appropriate to enable the couple to become familiar with the counselor and the setting. The counselor then asks if there is any information the couple needs in order to feel more comfortable; clients may want a further explanation of fees, to clarify the credentials of the counselor, to ask questions about the counseling process, or to raise concerns about confidentiality.

The counselor will undoubtedly need to collect more information. This is a good time to ask for specific and non-threatening data relating to length of marriage, length of time living together, whether or not this is a first marriage, age, and other information required for records. Then the counselor asks, "How do you feel about being here" This enables the clients to verbalize their anxieties and gives the counselor some sense of how prepared the couple is to get down to work.

```
Identify Current
Issues
(1.2)
```

The discussion about how the couple feels about being at counseling can smoothly lead to a description of the current presenting problem. It is vital that each partner have an opportunity to fully describe one's perspective without interference from the other. Throughout this process, it is the counselor's role to ensure that each partner feels one has had a full hearing. The counselor may feel that issues have not been equitably aired and encourage one partner to share additional information. When interruptions occur the counselor has an opportunity to demonstrate firm control of the situation in a gentle and understanding manner.

The couple usually comes to the first session with a burden of complaints and misunderstandings. What is most important is that each feels that both have aired the issues and have been understood by the counselor. There is seldom an attempt to resolve issues at this point, as there is so much pertinent information still to be collected. However, the counselor must give an indication that their difficulties are comprehended.

By directing general questions to both people the counselor can get a feeling for the interpersonal dynamics, such as who is dominant and takes the initiative.

Counselor: What brings you here today?

Joan: Our marriage feels empty. I've tried to figure out what is going on but I can't put my finger on any one issue. We're both going our own ways and we're losing a sense of being together.

Counselor: What made you decide on counseling?

Joan: I went to my family doctor because headaches and felt depressed.

Counselor: What did he say?

Joan: There wasn't anything physically wrong with me but he did ask me about our marriage. I told him I was bored with it and he suggested we seek counseling.

Paul: That's not quite true. There was a crisis of sorts—I don't know how you could forget.

Counselor: I want to understand this issue as each of you sees it, even though your versions are different. Now that Joan has started, let her continue. There will be lots of time for you, Paul, very soon.

Joan: We did have a big blow up two weeks ago, but that's not when it started. I was depressed long before that. The doctor had previously suggested counseling. I was thinking about it but hadn't mentioned it to Paul.... He wouldn't have discussed it anyway.

One possibility is already emerging. Not only are Joan and Paul failing to convey important personal information, but they each are feeling hurt, seeking revenge, and not communicating meaningfully. They are in the process of retreating into their own worlds. The counselor makes a tentative hypothesis that if their communication skills are strengthened, other areas of the relationship that are not yet too eroded will subsequently improve. It may be possible that Joan and Paul are cooperating to stay involved through their mutual hostility. This will be evidence of more strength in their relationship than if there was apathy.

Counselor: Could it be that you precipitated an argument with Paul so you could suggest getting professional help?

Joan: I hadn't thought about it that way, but it's probably true. I want something to happen.

Counselor: What have you tried?

Joan: I've thought of leaving, separation, but that doesn't seem to be an answer.

Counselor: Paul, how do you see the problem?

Paul: I've been trying to avoid the fact that there is one.

Counselor: Were you aware that Joan has considered separation?

Paul: She's threatened it when she's angry, but I didn't think she was serious.

Joan: That's one of the problems. You don't take me seriously.

Counselor: Joan, it's Paul turn to tell me about it. Paul, what else is a problem for you?

Paul: Joan has the baby and likes to be at home, at least she says she does. She's pretty self-sufficient. And when I get home I'm really tired. I work with people's problems all day, I'm a social worker, and I don't want more hassle as I walk in the door.

Counselor: Where do you feel the hassle?

Paul: Joan wants to tell me what went wrong, it seems as if there is a major complaint every day. She generally handles it competently so I don't see why we have to go over it again.

Counselor: And how do you respond?

Paul: Well, I listen to her while we eat dinner, then I watch TV or practice my music, or read. I need time to myself and she doesn't understand that.

Counselor: What's Joan doing at that time?

Paul: She practices her music, or visits her mother.

Counselor: Do you ever share your work day with Joan?

Paul: Once I leave the office I want to forget about it.

Joan: You want to forget about me all the time.

Paul: That's not true.

Counselor: It seems that underlying all of what you are both saying is a problem of communication—really being able to listen to one another or feeling that you have been understood. Before you leave today I will provide you with a very definite task to begin improving communication within an intimate relationship, but first, I can help you better if I have some more general information.

The counselor's tentative hypothesis is being born out: Paul and Joan are withdrawing from one another because the current form of their interaction is unpleasant; they operate as if they have no alternate communication skills. The counselor provides hope, first by acknowledging the problem, and second, by stating that there is an immediate direction in which they can begin to work.

**Discuss
Life Tasks**
(1.3)

A general view of each partner's coping skills as well as a broader data base can be quickly established by focusing on the major life tasks (Mosak, 1977). As members of the human community, all people must meet certain tasks which Adler described as society, work, and sex. The degree to which they feel they adequately deal with these tasks is a determinant of their sense of success in life overall. Many writers have further subdivided these tasks; those discussed in this first interview are Parenting, Work, Friends, Sex and Leisure (Dinkmeyer et al., 1979).

Discussing these life tasks with the couple can lend a note of optimism as they see that some areas of their relationship are successful. The counselor's role is to help the couple verbalize their own and the other's strengths and assets, some of which may never have been acknowledged throughout the relationship.

Counselor: There are a few areas of your life together I'd like to find out more about; this will help me in understanding your current situation. You said you have children.

Joan: Yes, two girls, ages four and eighteen months.

Oscar C. Christensen, Ed.D.

Counselor: Joan, how do you feel about your parenting?

Joan: I really enjoy the girls. I didn't think I would get such a kick out of being a mother after all of these years without children. I had two miscarriages before the eldest so I was convinced I'd never have children.

Counselor: What about you, Paul, how is parenting for you?

Paul: I don't have much time at home during the week when they are awake. I work with older kids and have never had much to do with little kids. It surprises me how much I want to do for them and with them. I really enjoy Saturday when Joan goes shopping and I have them all to myself.

As this process is an assessment technique, each task is only discussed briefly; the counselor must resist the temptation to get into fuller discussion. To do so results in slowing the pace and eliminating essential parts of the initial interview. The counselor needs to provide a comprehensive assessment and a feeling of closure for both the couple and the counselor. As the counselor explores each life style, mental notes are made on issues to be re-discussed at a later session.

At this point, the counselor's original hypothesis of possible strengths is confirmed. Both parents enjoy their roles and there is some cooperation between these roles. The counselor now assumes that the couple has tunnel vision; because they are feeling angry and hurt they are unable to acknowledge this relationship strength. This assumption will be checked out as soon as possible.

Counselor: As a social worker, what does your job entail?

Paul: I deal with teenagers who are identified as pre-delinquent.

Counselor: Do you enjoy the work?

Paul: Yes and no; I know I'm doing a good job-I can easily relate to that age group.

Counselor: And what's not so good about it?

Paul: I have an hour's drive each way; I've applied to an agency closer to home but I won't know about that for a few more weeks. Also, so many of the people I work with are really incompetent. They're nice people, but don't have a clue about kids.

Because Paul is so critical of his coworkers, he is possibly very critical of himself. The high standard he sets for himself may also be his expectation of Joan, and a clue to conflict to be investigated further.

Counselor: What about you, Joan, do you work outside the home?

Joan: I was a teacher and I really liked it but I want to be a full-time mother for now. I'll probably start substitute teaching when the youngest is in kindergarten.

Counselor: How do you feel about being at home full time?

Joan: There are so many things I like to do, such as sewing and interior decorating. It's nice to have time to pursue them. Besides, I know I'll be going back to work whenever I'm ready.

Both Joan's and Paul's individual sense of self-worth is another source of strength for the relationship. Joan is currently feeling satisfied as a mother and homemaker, and looks forward to pursuing her career when she is ready. Her sense of having her own life in order plus Paul's sense of doing a good job as a social worker will provide a solid foundation to work on their relationship.

Counselor: Do you each have individual friends as well as couple friends? (Silence) Joan, do you have friends of your own?

Joan: Since we've moved here I've found it hard to make new friends and my old ones are all in the city. It's too far to travel back and forth very often and phone calls are all long distance, so I'm losing touch. My mother has moved here too. She lives down the street, so I guess she's my best friend.

Counselor: Paul, what about you and friends?

Paul: My friends are mostly people I've worked with at one time or another, so I see them in professional situations, meetings and such. Once I've driven that hour home, I don't have much time or energy for friends during the week.

Counselor: Do you have couple friends?

Paul: I belong to a barbershop quartet and Joan sings with the Sweet Adelines so a lot of our weekend social time is spent there, either competing or practices or performances. So our joint contact is with these people, although we don't see them socially. There just isn't time.

Counselor: Do you entertain at home?

Joan: We used to when I was teaching but when I was pregnant I didn't feel up to it. Then when our first daughter was born there didn't seem to be time. We moved because we could afford a home out here but our friends don't want to drive this far. So we are losing touch.

Paul: That's not all of it. After guests would leave Joan always criticized me... always something I had done wrong.

Joan: You always made me feel uncomfortable. Sometimes you would hardly say a word all evening except "Can I get you another drink?" I had to keep the conversation going for both of us unless our guests were your work friends, and then all you talked about was cases and office gossip.

Both Joan and Paul are cooperating with the counselor in providing assessment information. Joan spontaneously begins to direct her comments to Paul. Both movements indicate a promise of cooperating to improve communication.

Counselor: How do you each feel about your sexual relationship?

Paul: It's almost nonexistent.

Counselor: Can you tell me more?

Paul: It was okay until the children were born, and then Joan was always too tired and now I've almost given up initiating anything because I'll be rejected.

Joan: To be honest, it was never that great, at least since we've been married. Before we were married we had so much fun, but it seemed that afterwards we had to settle down into being a properly married couple.

It would be tempting for the counselor to pursue this issue but to do so would mean eliminating other essential topics which need to be touched on. However, the couple needs reassurance that the sexual relationship will be dealt with soon, although not in this session. In spite of a culture that professes to treat sex openly, sexual interaction within a committed relationship is still a sensitive topic for most people. The counselor can follow up on this issue in a future session when a more solid relationship is established with the couple.

Counselor: We will certainly come back to this area, although not today. The basis of a healthy sexual relationship is good communication, so we'll work at that, then get back to your specific problems with sex. How do you spend your leisure time other than with the singing groups?

Joan: We both like to garden and we talk about our landscaping plans, but with only one salary we have to limit our spending.

Paul: Money does limit our leisure. We used to travel during school holidays and I'd save up my overtime. Joan manages the money—she's good at budgeting. We have a camper so we'll go camping this summer.

Joan: Paul and I have a good time traveling. He plans interesting side trips. We do a lot of exploring and he turns a very ordinary trip into an adventure. When I think about it, we don't fight so much when we travel.

Counselor: You have learned to cooperate on money management and traveling. It's my guess you can use those same skills to advantage in other areas too.

The presence of many couple strengths has been affirmed. Joan and Paul have not been able to acknowledge these because they are so involved in being angry for being excluded from each other's lives. The process of verbalizing these assets helps them to begin to recognize aspects of their relationship they have been able to build together. The counselor's continued encouragement provides a sense of optimism of where counseling can lead them.

> # Establish
> # Commitment
> ## (1.4)

At this point it is essential to clearly determine that the goals of the counselor and of each partner are congruent, even if on a short term basis. Often couples are afraid to make a long term commitment to working on their relationship because they cannot foresee that the changes will be sufficient. But even in the most painful relationships, if a couple comes once for counseling, they are likely to be prepared to make a commitment to work together for one week. If they are not, then counseling for separation may be a more appropriate goal.

Counselor: I am assuming that because you are here, you want to work on your marriage. Is that true for you, Joan?

Joan: I think I do, but I'm not really sure.

Counselor: Would you be prepared to work on your marriage for one week? You would return a week from today and let me know if you are open to continuing marriage counseling.

Joan: Yes, I'm prepared to do that.

Counselor: And Paul, do you wish to work on this relationship?

Paul: Definitely, that's why I'm here.

Enabling the couple to hear one another make this commitment, no matter how short ranged, clearly provides some hope for directions counseling can take. To not have the commitment invites sabotage of any tasks assigned to be completed outside of the office setting. Even where the relationship is in greater jeopardy than seems to be the case here, once the couple has made any degree of commitment the counselor would assign the following exercise, as talking together in a novel structure can relieve much of the tension between the couple and pave the way for more productive counseling. In the event that there is not an agreement to proceed in marital counseling, either or both spouses may be referred for individual counseling. On occasion, individual counseling can be a useful adjunct to marital adjustment or separation.

**Assign Homework
(Couple Conference)**

(1.5)

Counselor: One of your main problems seems to be communication. In one way or another this is a basic issue for most couples I see. I am going to outline a structure for listening and talking to each other, then we will see if you are prepared to follow it for only two hours in the next week.

At the same time as the counselor is explaining the structure, the counselor is writing the instructions out and will give the paper to the couple to take home. The reason for the counselor doing the writing is so that the partners cannot blame one another for any misunderstandings that may arise. In later sessions the couple will be asked to assume more responsibility for taking instructions by writing such directions themselves.

Like many couples, Joan and Paul have not made time to talk together; when they do talk they have learned to stay with safe topics and evade potentially volatile or sensitive issues. The high degree of structure of the couple conference provides a built-in, protective device, imposed by the counselor. The purpose of the couple conference is to allow the couple to express literally anything they wish to at a time when they are not in conflict. Once these issues have been aired, they are most likely to be able to deal with present concerns.

Counselor: This is called a Couple Conference. You will take two, one-hour time periods. In each, one of you will speak for half an hour, while the other only listens, that is, makes no response at all. In the second half hour, the other speaks, and the first listens. This means, of course, that the second person has an opportunity for rebuttal. However, in the second one-hour conference, the second speaker from the first conference will speak first. The topics may include anything you want... how you feel about life in general, the past, the future, what is currently going on... anything.

Joan: I couldn't talk for a whole half hour.

Counselor: You don't have to talk all the time. Silences are okay. How often have either of you, throughout your whole relationship, had the opportunity to say anything you want, knowing the other person is prepared to listen?

Paul: We always seem to be competing for time when we do talk. We jump in and contradict each other.

Counselor: Now you have a chance to think about how you want to phrase it. If you say anything, and as you hear yourself, ask, "Is this what I intended to say?" You can take the statement back and change it around.

Joan: But what if I say all I want in the first ten minutes?

Counselor: You two have not been communicating effectively for a long time. So once you have dealt with the first issues, ask yourself, "What have I wanted to say to Paul over the years?" Think about it. My experience with couples is that they fill up the silences pretty quickly. It is essential that you do not cut the time short; take the full half hour each. Often to person who is most reluctant to talk will change the time rule and the other is afraid to express his or her need. Some other guidelines are important. Set up a time when there will be no interruptions—take the phone off the hook, be sure your children are sound asleep or arrange a babysitter, and go out. Do not have the conference while you are driving.

The counselor continues to include every detail of these instructions on the written sheet. Couples appear to have greater success with their couple conference when they have a "tailor-made" guideline being developed just for them, compared with a prepared handout.

Paul: This is beginning to sound interesting.

Counselor: If you can enjoy doing this, that is a bonus. Another guideline is that you sit back to back. You are both so used to misreading each other's body language and facial expression that for now I want you to concentrate on listening and talking. When you come to the end of the hour, STOP! Don't carry on beyond the hour. Change your activity, perhaps make some coffee.

Joan: There sure are a lot of rules.

Counselor: The guidelines are specifically designed to enable you to talk without falling into old patterns which have become destructive and ineffective. The rules are to protect you and get you started in a more positive direction. Once you have successfully completed a conference, you may feel differently about each other. Are you willing to do this twice in the next week?

Joan: Yes, it sounds good. We have nothing to lose.

Counselor: What about you, Paul?

Paul: Absolutely.

Because they were asked to do the couple conference immediately after they had committed themselves to working on the relationship, it is unlikely that the couple will disagree to work on the exercise. The counselor's credibility, combined with a warm concerned approach will lead couples who truly care about the relationship to trust in this professional advice. If one partner were to disagree with the couple conference, counseling would move in the direction of investigating the resistance.

Counselor: To ensure that you get right down to work we will set up two conferences for the coming week now; you are, in effect, making appointments with one another that are as important to keep as the ones you make with me. If you find you have to change the time or place, make the specific change and write it down, making sure your partner knows about the change. When will you have the first conference? It's a good idea to have several days between them. (The time, date, and place for each conference is then discussed and noted on the counselor's written instructions, which are then handed to the couple.) If there are any complications or misunderstandings after the first conference, please call me so we can clear up difficulties immediately.

(This message also models for the couple that when something bothersome comes up, they are to deal with it immediately.)

> **Examine
> Disturbing
> Elements in Self**
> (1.6)

Husbands and wives who are having problems in their marriage are often disturbed by unexpressed feelings they are experiencing. To each partner it may appear that the other has few painful feelings, such as remorse or guilt. They rarely talk about personal discomfort. Instead, they try to establish blame and are not ready to hear what the other is also experiencing. Once mutually painful feelings are shared, much to their surprise, couples are more ready to move towards each other.

Counselor: As I listen to you today, I sense that you both have some pretty uncomfortable feelings about yourselves that you have been unable to express. (The counselor continues explaining this only until there is a sign of recognition from one of the partners, who is then asked directly about the discomfort.) Paul, do you recognize such feelings ?

Paul: As Joan harps on me for drawing in and not talking to her I feel myself withdrawing more and more. She thinks I do it because I don't care about her. But that's not true. I feel

Oscar C. Christensen, Ed.D.

so lonely and I can't respond to her anger. I know if I say something it will be destructive. I need to protect myself, so I don't say anything.

Counselor: The lonelier you feel the less you can respond.

Paul: I feel as if nobody cares about me.

Joan: When this happens, when I get so impatient because he won't talk... he just sits and watches TV or puts the stereo headphones on and cuts me out... my voice gets shriller. You know, I want to shut up but I can't stop. I hear myself shouting horrible things, anything to get a response. I want to hit him... at least I don't do that. But I feel like a shrew and I detest myself.

Counselor: You're hating what you hear yourself doing, but you can't get it turned around.

This discussion will continue until the feelings are clarified. At future sessions there will be an opportunity to deal with the issues that have surfaced. In the meantime this awareness that the other partner is undergoing pain seems to preclude them feeling that they have to keep testing the injury to see if it still hurts.

> **Present Diagnostic Hypotheses**
> (1.7)

The couple who comes for counseling may feel desperate about their situation and need a lot of encouragement. They depend heavily on the counselor's assessment in order to regain faith in their own ability to bring about change. That they have agreed upon a couple conference indicates their willingness to begin to move in a positive direction.

The previous interchange further confirms that as the couple attempts to deal with issues, they create even more distance between one another; they have run out of skills that would enable them to move in a more positive direction. As Paul withdraws, Joan attacks; as she attacks, he withdraws further. In her frustration Joan feels impotent and intensifies her response to overcome her sense of futility.

The diagnostic hypothesis is a summation of the problem and an overview of the next few sessions. It includes the counselor's prognosis which must contain an encouraging element such as, "The very fact that you are here means that you are prepared to work together."

The counselor then asks the couple to establish four more weekly appointments. At the end of this set, the counselor and the couple may arrange further weekly or biweekly appointments. It is strongly recommended that future sessions be recorded, the couple providing their own cassette tape to listen to at home between appointments.

Session Two

```
Discuss
Homework
(2.1)
```

After a brief period of getting settled, the counselor asks, "How were the couple conferences?" The assumption that the two planned conferences were carried out demonstrates the counselor's faith in both the couple conference as a tool and the couple's commitment. Either partner may respond. (If the homework was not completed, the couple's resistance or sabotage efforts must be carefully analyzed and the value of each partner's commitment to the relationship reassessed.)

Joan: Well, they were okay. I had to speak first and that was difficult. I had no idea what Paul was thinking. When I spoke last it was much easier. But, yet....

Counselor: You seem to have some reservations about it.

Joan: It was so different. I felt pressure on me. It was the first time I've told Paul calmly that I often think of leaving.

Counselor: How did you feel about yourself after you had finished speaking?

Joan: Pretty good, I guess. When I thought about it, we hadn't just talked for an hour for years. That's been the problem. Paul lectures when he has something to say.

Counselor: And how did you feel about Paul after the conference?

Joan:	It's been so long since we've talked. He said a lot of things that I haven't heard before, things I wish he'd said earlier. After all this time of waiting for him to say them, I'm afraid they may not be true. I'm afraid to trust him.
Counselor:	What kinds of things?
Joan:	Particularly how much he loves me... how important I am to him. Why would he say this now that he wants me to stay, and wouldn't tell me before?
Counselor:	Perhaps Paul can answer that.
Paul:	I've been telling her through....
Counselor:	Turn to Joan and tell her directly.

The purpose of this analysis is so that each partner can realize the value of the effort that the other put into the couple conference, and the satisfaction it provided. They have previously taken for granted that each will know how the other feels. This interchange, then, is also the beginning of teaching each partner to check out assumptions within a very personal context.

Counselor:	I've thought I've said them through the things I do for you. I'm always honest with you. I get so busy, there never seems to be an opportunity... you always are so busy with the girls.... I guess I'm making excuses. I find it almost impossible to say what I really feel, and now that you've said you might leave, and I'm telling you, you won't believe me.

The conferences provide a context in which you can say what you've found so difficult previously.

Paul:	I guess I've got nothing to lose.
Counselor:	How did you find the conference format?
Paul:	Really hard. I can't stand not getting immediate feedback.
Counselor:	How has immediate feedback helped your discussions before?
Paul:	I guess it's cut them off. We argue, or I shut up, then there's no discussion at all.
Counselor:	How did you feel about yourself during the conference?
Paul:	It was so hard to keep talking, although there was lots I wanted to say.

Counselor: Perhaps you wanted immediate feedback so you wouldn't have to keep talking and say those things that are so difficult for you.

Paul: You mean, if Joan talks that lets me off the hook? I guess so.

Counselor: And how do you feel now that you have spent a whole hour doing your own talking?

Paul: Freed up. I'm going to have to work at it so it comes more naturally.

Counselor: It seems you are both saying that although the conference was initially uncomfortable, you gained from it. A conference is only a tool, one means of getting communication moving when you reach a block. Just as you choose a specific tool for a specific purpose, you can to choose a conference to improve communication. Is this a tool you would agree to use in the future?

Paul: Yes, I would.

Joan: Me too.

Counselor: Then would you also agree that whenever one of you wishes to call a conference, the other will agree to attend?

Joan: Certainly.

Paul: Fine with me.

This couple is discovering what most couples who have couple conferences soon learn: the trouble in their relationship is not because one of them is sick or to blame. The cause of the problem is that they have not learned to deal with conflict and to apply skills which can help to keep them working closely together and hence create intimacy. Whether or not they maintain intimacy will depend on the degree to which they will each take responsibility for initiating whatever technique seems applicable. Here, the counselor models establishing a contract for future, similar issues.

> **Assign Homework**
> **(Couple Conference)**
> **(2.2)**

Counselor: You both still have lots to discuss. Your homework for this week is for each of you to spontaneously call a conference. Some further guidelines are these: The person who calls the conference speaks first. Leave a few hours between calling the conference and actually having it. When you call a conference, establish at that time where and when it will be.

Reidentify Current Issues (2.3)

Current issues include anything that has happened since the previous session or issues from the past not aired in the first session. A question such as "Is there anything I should know about that we did not discuss last week?" may elicit such information as previous separations, affairs, concerns about extended family members, or any pressures on the couple from within the community. Many times a couple will give a rundown of their week. This is appropriate, providing they do not ramble on, as it gives the counselor further insight into the interrelationship dynamics, as well as an opportunity to point out relationship strengths that the couple takes for granted. The counselor may choose to assign relevant homework which applies to one aspect of a current Issue.

At this time the counselor clarifies that if either partner wants an individual session, that person can ask for it. There may be anger and frustration at the other partner that needs venting. Because of fear of inflicting pain or fear of retaliation, these feelings may not be fully expressed unless an individual session is scheduled.

Assess Family Constellation (2.4)

The couple is now ready to work at understanding unique characteristics that each brought to the marriage, and how these can enhance or disturb the relationship. The initial step is for the counselor to gather information about both family constellations, including how many brothers and sisters each has and how many years younger or older they are than the client. It is important to include children who died, whether in childbirth or later. If the client is aware of a miscarriage, this is pertinent too. Then the counselor asks for three outstanding characteristics of each sibling and of oneself; "What kind of a child were you, as you saw yourself through the eyes of that eight or nine-year-old Paul?" "What was your older brother like as you remember him?"

Present Diagnostic Hypotheses
(2. 5)

The implications of family constellation for revealing dynamics of a couple's relationship are invaluable. The counselor who needs more information is directed to Forer (1976). Once basic data is collected, the couple is given immediate feedback.

Counselor: Joan, as the eldest of three children you say you were responsible and organized and took on much of the management of the household. Paul, you were the youngest of two. Your sister was bossy and tried to manage you, and you decided early that nobody was going to tell you what to do, least of all your older sister. How did you handle your sister when she tried to manage you?

Paul: I learned to keep out of her path so she couldn't get her hands on me.

Counselor: I wonder if, when you feel Joan is making demands on you, you use some of those same techniques?

This discussion will continue, with the counselor pointing out possible conflicts and how each is responding to the other based on similar responses made to siblings, especially the sibling in the same constellation position as the partner.

When each partner is in the same constellation position, for example if both are youngest children, intense competition or frustration may develop. As one woman said, "My husband and I are both youngest children... neither of us wants to make a final decision on anything. Once we discovered that this is often a characteristic of youngest children, we stopped having unrealistic expectations of one another's decision making. What we've learned is that if neither of us makes a decision, either somebody else will make it for us or, over time, a decision doesn't matter anyway."

As the discussion proceeds and areas of conflict are identified, the counselor asks for a recent, specific incident that illustrates that point.

Counselor: Paul, when did you most recently sense that Joan was making a demand on you?

Paul: Last night. She wants us to settle our holiday plans and because of the new position I've applied for, I can't give her a specific time.

Counselor: Would you and Joan reenact that discussion now? Go back to last night and pretend you are having that interchange for the first time. Joan, you begin. What did you need to know?

The couple replay the demand-conflict situation. Upon completion, the counselor asks in what way they are arguing based on how arguments went in their family of origin. Then the counselor asks them to reenact the situation but this time as they would like it to be. The ensuing discussion will focus on how they can use their new knowledge about their family constellations to facilitate growth, and to move them closer to one another.

Every position within the family constellation can have an advantage. The counselor must help the couple perceive their own and their partner's strengths as complementary factors rather than as opposing forces. There is a wealth of information in even the briefest family constellation outline and this discussion will continue until at least the end of this second session.

As the termination time approaches, the counselor provides encouragement to the couple by summarizing the strengths that have been evident during the session, then reconfirms the time and date of the next session.

Session Three

> ### Discuss Homework
> (3.1)

The first item for discussion is homework. Whether or not the couple did it, successes or problems they had with it, and how they felt about it provide immediate and valuable information. Again the counselor assumes the couple did the assignment. If they did not, their method of avoidance points out who is likely to be sabotaging counseling, what it is they fear, or who has less of an investment in working at improving the marriage. If the "spontaneous" couple conferences were not held, the reasons and each partner's feelings about it must be carefully explained without laying blame. This provides the counselor with an excellent opportunity to model discussing something that did not work without having to find fault, and to gently dissuade each partner from falling into the blame-finding trap. The dynamics of this process are overt and provide protection for each partner, especially the one who may tend to feel blamed or guilty. The counselor then asks, "What do you intend to do about it?" and a commitment is made to either do the homework or not do it. This agreement to not do something is generally a new and stimulating concept; it entails not being disappointed by unfulfilled expectations, and being totally honest about one's true intentions.

Structure Couple Communication (3.2)

Throughout this and successive sessions, the counselor focuses on another element of communication in an intimate relationship, taking responsibility for one's own feelings. A structured exercise, "I feel...," which can be taught to couples privately or in a group session is thoroughly outlined in Hawes (1982). The essence of the message to each partner is:

Counselor: Each of you has both different and similar feelings about the same issue. Your feelings belong to you, and whatever your feelings are at any given moment, they are yours representing your personal reality. These feelings are not to be evaluated or questioned by anyone else, and do not need to be justified by you. You make a choice about how you feel in a given situation based on your belief about that situation. And you must respect your partner's right to choose one's feelings and responses.

The following excerpt is based on a spontaneous couple conference that went well.

Oscar C. Christensen, Ed.D.

Counselor: I'm feeling curious about your couple conference this week.

Joan: For me they were good; I'm able to tell Paul things that I haven't been able to express before and now that he is listening I feel much closer to him. He's still reluctant to talk though.

Paul: What makes you say that?

Joan: When I called the conference first, you couldn't settle on a time and then when you had your half hour you just dealt with responding to what I had discussed. You didn't bring up anything new, did you?

Paul: There you go, making assumptions about me.

Joan: You didn't add any new information. What else was I supposed to think?

Paul: You could think that I'm trying instead of getting so upset.

Counselor: Let's stop here. Would you be willing to go over this discussion again, with some new ground rules? (Both nod assent.) Almost any time we ask a question, especially in an intimate relationship, we receive a defensive re response. If you say, "Why are you late?" perhaps your partner hears a criticism, "How could you inconvenience me this way?" and responds with a statement that either increases hostility, "I never said I'd be home at a specific time" or pacifies you, "I'm sorry, traffic was really heavy," rather than honestly respond to the question. But your partner may have meant something else, for example, "I was worried about you," or "I have cooked your favorite casserole and now it's mushy" or any number of possibilities.

Counselor: You may remember that I began this discussion with a statement that began with "I feel...," "I'm feeling curious about your couple conference this week." Joan, you responded immediately with how it was for you. I didn't need to ask a question to get a response. Then within six statements you asked three questions, all of which received defensive answers. As well, you both decided how the other was feeling, then responded as if your supposition were true.

Counselor: From here on, every time one of you expresses a feeling, before you go any further with the content, allow time for your partner to check out the feeling. This means that each time one of you says, "I feel...," the message is a red flag that the other will respond by inviting an explanation of the feeling. I began the discussion with "I'm feeling curious about your couple conference this week."

Joan: Oh! I think I said... they were good for me. I like being able to tell Paul things I couldn't express before. Now he's listening to me I feel much closer to him. But he's still reluctant to say...

Counselor: Now you are telling Paul how he is feeling.

Joan: I'm not sure how to change that.

Counselor: Put it into a framework of your own feelings and see what happens.

Joan: I feel much closer to you. But I'm uneasy when I think you don't want to say something to me, yet it is on your mind.

Paul: When I'm having to really think about us, I don't want to say what isn't true. So I need lots of space. Why did you...? Oh, that's a question. I wonder what I did that made you feel uneasy.

Counselor: Well done, Paul. You caught your question and converted it to a statement about yourself.

This exercise is deceptively simple. Even highly motivated couples such as Joan and Paul have to work very hard to change their language habits; they need monitored practice plus much support, encouragement, and modeling from the counselor. Couples who do decide to eliminate questions and implement "I feel..." messages report a major improvement in intimate communication.

Joan: When I called the conference, you said you agreed to have it that night, but you would rather not set the time until after dinner.

Paul: That was because I didn't know how tired I'd be.

Joan: It would really help me if you said that at the time. Well, then when you had your half hour, you didn't bring up any new information, and it seemed that you couldn't be bothered....

Counselor: Try rewording that.

Joan: Oh, this is hard! When you didn't bring up any new information, I felt disappointed.

Counselor: Now that you have given a feeling, wait for Paul to respond to it.

Paul: (long pause) So, I've got to check out the feeling. Why were you disappointed?

Counselor: Now you have a question. Tell me about feeling disappointed.

Joan: My interpretation was that the conference didn't mean as much to you as it did to me, so you wouldn't give it much thought beforehand.

Paul: That's not it at all. We've had several of these now within a short time, and I find it easier to respond to you. I was running out of topics. And I feel threatened.

Joan: (long pause) Oh! I'm getting the hang of this now. Tell me about feeling threatened.

This discussion carried on until both felt comfortable with their new communication technique.

Counselor: I feel good.

Paul: Tell me about feeling good.

Counselor: You're both learning this quickly and applying it appropriately to the situation. I am going to give you another homework assignment, again for one week only.

Paul: Good, this is really helping.

```
┌─────────────────────────┐
│        Assign           │
│      Homework           │
│        (3.3)            │
└─────────────────────────┘
```

Counselor: During the next week, omit asking each other any questions. Have fun with it. Don't even ask, "What time is it?" Play with language and turn all questions into statements. At the same time, practice giving "I feel" messages, then wait for an invitation to continue with an explanation of your feeling. Each of you give at least five "I feel" messages a day. These can be positive statements as well, such as "I feel excited," or "content" and so forth.

> ## Reidentify
> ## Current Issues
> ### (3.4)

The counselor asks, "What else do you want to deal with to-day?" to again provide an opportunity for the couple to discuss current issues. By this time they have probably discovered that what they had originally presented as the main issue is a manifestation of the basic problem that stems from a lack of understanding of the dynamics of the relationship and from a lack of communication skills. Hence, they are prepared to be open to what the counselor has to offer. However, if the couple does have an issue, they will not feel comfortable until they have it aired. Before counseling can progress, the problem must be addressed, or assurance given that it will be dealt with in a reasonable time.

> ## Discuss
> ## Expectations of
> ## Men, Women,
> ## and Marriage
> ### (3.5)

The expectation one has of a husband or wife is closely aligned, either in similarity or opposition, to the earliest perceptions one had of men and women as exemplified by a mother and father, or their surrogates. To the child, the situation at home represents the whole world and so the relationship between parents appears as the only possible one between men and women (Dreikurs, 1946). Partners are not generally aware of the source of their expectations as it has been camouflaged by a more sophisticated current view of one's parents, by family stories, or by having a purpose in remembering parents in a way that aligns with a chosen view. It is possible to overcome this subterfuge by asking each partner separately, "As a small child, how did you view your mother?" "Through the eyes of that little child you once were, what was your father like?" "As you were growing up, what were your thoughts about your parents' marriage relationship?"

This brief data gathering is a broadening of the family constellation information from the previous session, and must be viewed by the counselor as completing the whole.

> **Present
> Diagnostic
> Hypotheses**
>
> (3.6)

Counselor: Joan, as the eldest child you modeled your behavior very much on the way you perceived your mother, although you didn't often feel as secure as she seemed. The fact that you trusted her so much made modeling easier. At the same time, your father was there for fun. Did you expect Paul to be your source of fun?

Joan: Absolutely. I'm very serious, like my mother. I find it difficult to initiate fun myself.

Counselor: You say your father really put himself out for his family, for example, he would go on picnics even though he didn't like them?

Joan: Once he got there, he would be playful with us.

Counselor: I wonder what went on between your parents for him to get there.

Joan: They never communicated conflict, but my guess now, as a grownup, is that he went there to appease my mother.

Counselor: Of course, you were not aware of that at the time. Yet we all make assumptions based on our subjective reality of the moment, and act on these as if they were so. I wonder what this tells you about your relationship with Paul.

Joan: I expect him to be fun and easygoing, and to put himself out for me because I saw my father that way. But that wasn't the way it was, really, for Dad. And even though Paul can be fun, it's unrealistic of me to expect that as a constant from him. I'm anticipating behavior from him that just does not fit.

This discussion will continue until the end of the session, and perhaps over to subsequent sessions as well.

As the session draws to a close, the counselor provides encouragement by giving recognition to observable, forward movement in the relationship.

Session Four

```
Discuss
Homework
(4.1)
```

Counselor: I feel interested.

Joan: Why?

Paul: I get it. Tell me about feeling interested.

Counselor: You had a difficult homework task, to entirely avoid questions. I'm wondering how it went

Paul: We are certainly talking more. We forgot and asked questions a few times. It was impossible not to, but we were very aware of them being questions that were appropriate to the situation. So it injected a humorous note.

Joan: What I'm discovering is that we can discuss serious topics, yet not take ourselves too seriously. Having to acknowledge feelings, both my own and Paul's, is making our talking much warmer. I don't feel that I'm at him, and uptight a much. But there is something else I'd like to talk about today.

Counselor: Go ahead.

Joan: We are doing much better with our communications, but do we have to call a conference every time we want to bring up a new issue?

Counselor: The couple conference is only a tool. If the issue is large or potentially explosive, the structure of the conference provides a safeguard. There are many other ways. What do you have in mind?

Joan: I don't want to nag or yell, but there are other things I want changed, and I don't know how to introduce them.

Counselor: Give me an example.

Joan: I want Paul to do more around the house without me asking.

Paul: I don't mind you asking.

Joan:	But I don't want to ask. If I ask, you are doing it for me, and I want you to do it because it needs doing. I don't want to have to thank you for helping. It makes me feel beholden .
Paul:	Tell me about feeling beholden.
Joan:	If you do something for me, than I think I owe you a favor. When we were both working we shared the chores. Now I do all of the housework.
Paul:	I put the children to bed, and I bathe them, when I'm home.
Joan:	I want to put them to bed sometimes too, without having to do the dinner clean up as well.

> **Discuss**
> **Marriage**
> **Council I**
> (4.2)

Counselor:	Your methods of problem solving have improved immeasurably in the past four weeks. Joan, you are able to express your problems as ones you own, and Paul, you are not tuning out when you feel the heat. You are not going to want to spend your appointment time looking at these kinds of issues separately, so I'm proposing a strategy which I label a marriage council. You establish a regular weekly meeting time at which you discuss contentious issues. When something comes up during the week that bothers you, you both know that you will have an opportunity to discuss it at a time when the other person is prepared to listen. At the meeting you say it once and then you don't feel you are continuously shooing flies.
Paul:	We save all of our complaints for that time?
Counselor:	It's not just for complaints; it's for all the topics you don't get around to during the week, possibly because you are tired or busy. These include planning fun, deciding gifts, sharing fantasies, the list is endless. Some couples use it for deciding major issues such as birth control, taking courses, and career changes. Recording minutes helps remind you of decisions made. One couple started these

meetings before their marriage and all these years later have a written history of their relationship which is their priceless possession.

Joan: This is a good idea.

Paul: It sounds like what we need.

Counselor: Would you be prepared to have one this week so that we could review it next session?

**Assign Homework
(Marriage Council)**

(4.3)

The marriage council becomes the homework for the following week. The day and time are set in the counselor's office so that as soon as the couple leaves they can immediately plan topics to work on. The counselor is still taking responsibility for structuring situations. Because Joan is trying so hard not to impose her managing on Paul, and he is still finding it difficult to initiate, they may arrive at an impasse, not have the marriage council, and then each blame the other for lack of movement. To date, they have both undertaken all assignments, learned from then, and instituted them in their regular routine. The counselor fully expects that their relationship will be further enhanced by the marriage council; then Joan will be organizing where it is appropriate and Paul will take more initiative for action.

**Reidentify
Current
Issues**

(4.4)

These are discussed in the same mode as in previous sessions.

> ### Describe Early Recollections
> (4 5)

Early recollections are regarded as a prototype of an individual's fundamental attitudes (Adler, 1969; Ijams, 1989). Although these attitudes are predominantly unconscious perceptions of the environment and the individual's role in the world, the individual nevertheless operates in accordance with this attitudinal frame of reference (Mosak, 1972). Hence, early recollections of both partners provide valuable information .

> ### Present Diagnostic Hypothesis
> (4.6)

The counselor obtains three early recollections from each partner (Dinkmeyer et al., 1979, p. 88). Interpretations are made, then a discussion ensues on how this information describes the current modus vivendi. Presented with these insights, the couple can understand where and how they can cooperate more efficiently, stop competing with one another, and interpret previous data in terms of the strengths and assets of the relationship.

Session Five

By the fifth session, a pattern has developed for marriage counseling which is followed in successive sessions.

> ### Discuss Homework
> (5.1)

In this fifth session, the couple discusses the institution of the marriage council. Any difficulties or misunderstandings are clarified; occasionally a new homework assignment will emanate from this. Then the couple can decide if they want to make marriage councils, perhaps in a more personalized format, a part of their weekly routine.

> ### Reidentify
> ### Current
> ### Issues
> (5.2)

During this section the counselor will assign pertinent homework. Rather than the very structured assignments to date, the homework can be an outgrowth from the answer to "What would you like to do about that?" or "What would you like to ask of your partner for one week only?" This latter question must be asked of both partners.

> ### Describe First
> ### Impressions of a
> ### Relationship
> (5.3)

The early recollections of a marriage (Belove, 1980), although not as valid as life style early recollections, provide understanding of the deterioration of the relationship. This knowledge can lead to greater acceptance of the current dilemma, and thereby greater impetus for improvement.

Counselor: Paul, remember the very first time you set eyes on Joan. What did you notice?

Paul: My friend and I were at a Sweet Adeline concert; she had a lovely smile and was a lively leader of her group. My friend knew her and said he would arrange a date.

Counselor: And the next time..., what did you notice then?

Paul: I was standing in her apartment lobby and she literally bounced out of the elevator. She was so confident.

Counselor: Anything else that appealed to you at that moment?

Paul: As we walked to the car, she chattered away. We had arranged ranged to go to a movie but she was excited about a group at a local club. Before we knew it she had us organized to go there. It was a particularly good group and a fun evening.

Counselor: What is it you most often complain about Joan these days?

Paul: Oh no! Her demands and getting everyone organized and wanting to do things when I want to be quiet and alone.

A similar discussion goes on with Joan, who remembers that Paul was quiet, yet she was impressed with his firmness. She recognized that the fun she originally saw in him was most often in response to activities that she set up.

> ## Present Diagnostic Hypotheses
> (5.4)

These impressions and their relevance to the present situation are discussed further. The counselor points out how the characteristics each valued most in the other have now taken on negative connotations. In making suggestions about turning the negative views to the positive, the counselor teaches the couple to do likewise. While still in the office setting and with the counselor's guidance, they may reevaluate perspectives of several situations, deciding what they will choose to look at differently.

> ## Contract for More Sessions
> (5.5)

This session is the last of the four that were contracted at the end of the first interview. Now it is time to arrange further sessions, either as a block or one at a time. The couple chooses whether to meet weekly, biweekly, or monthly. The length of each session may range from one to three hours according to issues to be addressed. The couple is thereby involved in establishing their ongoing counseling needs.

Now that the couple has a firmer grasp of communication skills and a deeper understanding of the dynamics of their relationship, it is appropriate to begin working on other issues, particularly the sexual one. For this, the counselor is directed to Evans and Evans (1989) for an education program from an Adlerian perspective. Counseling will continue until the couple decides that they no longer require it.

As an adjunct to counseling, the couple may be referred to a couple enrichment workshop or study group (Hawes, 1982), to be attended either concurrently with counseling or at a later date. This is an opportunity for them to learn further communication skills for an intimate relationship. They will also realize that they are not alone in having to apply themselves to working at a committed relationship if it is to be as stimulating and rewarding as they undoubtedly expected their marriage to be.

The Adlerian model of marriage counseling has several distinctive features. It is initially highly structured with the counselor directing the educational process after receiving a commitment from each partner to work on the relationship.

By agreeing to participate in the sessions, the couple takes the initiative for bringing forward their intimate problems and working them through in the context provided by the counselor. The structured process gives the couple effective techniques for creating warmth and understanding, and hence an openness to recognizing new solutions to old problems. They respond by gradually assuming responsibility for their own communication and problem-solving efforts. At the same time, the structure provides a safeguard against falling back into old, destructive patterns. The concept of ongoing encouragement is important. Strengths and assets are continually noted as well as the couple's competent use of newly learned skills.

The Adlerian marriage counselor models and teaches mutual respect, cooperative decision making, equality in relationships, and relinquishment of unchecked assumptions. The counselor thus provides the couple with an opportunity to experience he value of immediate expression of feelings, positive feedback, following through on commitments, and creative approaches to problems which seemed unsolvable. The counselor and the couple are working toward the mutually agreed upon goal of maintaining and improving a relationship This is a continuing process of (communication that will enhance not only the marriage but the individuals within it. It is the Adlerian counselor's optimism and belief in the ability of people to acquire new relationship skills that allows for renewal and growth within the existing relationship.

References

Adler, A. (1969). *The science of living.* Garden City, NY: Anchor Books-Doubleday.

Belove, L. (1980). First encounters of the close kind (FECK): The use of the story of the first interaction as an early recollection of a marriage. *Journal of Individual Psychology, 36*(2), 191-208.

Dinkmeyer, D.C., Pew, W.L., & Dinkmeyer, D.C., Jr. (1979). *Adlerian counseling and psychology.* Monterey, CA: Brooks/Cole.

Dreikurs, R. (1946). *The challenge of marriage.* New York: Hawthorn Books, Inc.

Evans, C.D., & Evans, R.R. (1989). Working with remarried couples. In. R.M. Kern, E.C. Hawes, & O.C. Christensen (Eds.). *Couples therapy: An Adlerian perspective.* Minneapolis, MN: Educational Media.

Forer, L. (1976). *The birth order factor.* New York: Pocket Books.

Hawes, E.C. (1982). *Couples growing together.* Wooster, OH: The Social Interest Press.

Ijams, M. (1989). Lifestyle of a relationship. In. R.M. Kern, E.C. Hawes, & O.C. Christensen (Eds.). *Couples therapy: An Adlerian perspective.* Minneapolis, MN: Educational Media.

Mosak, H.H. (1972). *Early recollections as a projective technique.* Chicago: Alfred Adler Institute.

Mosak, H.H. (1977). *On purpose. Collected papers.* Chicago: Alfred Adler Institute.

Shulman, B.H. (1973). *Contributions to individual psychology: Selected papers.* Chicago: Alfred Adler Institute.

Stewart, N.R., Winborn, R.B., Johnson, R.G., Burks, H.M. Jr.,& Engelkes, J.R. (1978). *Systematic counseling.* Englewood Cliffs, NJ: Prentice-Hall.

Oscar C. Christensen, Ed.D.

Chapter 7

Parent Study Groups

by Gary D. McKay
and Joyce McKay

This chapter is dedicated to Rudolf Dreikurs, M.D. whose work has provided encouragement to millions of parents and teachers. Those of us who have carried on his work, owe a great debt to "Dr. D."

Introduction

The purpose of this chapter is to provide the reader with a comprehensive and practical orientation to the organization of parent study groups. This chapter will include a detailed description of the parent study group process, including essential leader characteristics and relevant materials.

Basic Elements of Parent Study Groups

A parent study group is a series of regular meetings of parents with a leader, who together study Adlerian principles as they apply to parent-child relationships. They are educational groups, as opposed to therapy experiences. Therefore parent study groups take the form of courses in parenthood. These groups usually meet once a week for a specified number of sessions. Usually, the groups study specific Adlerian materials such as *Children: The Challenge* (Dreikurs & Soltz, 1964), *Raising a Responsible Child* (Dinkmeyer & McKay, 1973), and *Systematic Training for Effective Parenting (STEP)* (Dinkmeyer & McKay, 1989). Later, we'll describe each of these Adlerian parent education programs.

Between meetings, participants are expected to read material from the assigned Adlerian text and practice the principles they are learning in their families.

Parent study groups help parents learn how to establish democratic relationships with their children. While some parents do learn new skills from simply reading books on parenting, the value of the group experience permits parents to exchange ideas and questions, and to receive support and encouragement.

Parent study groups have been conducted in a variety of settings. School counselors offer parent study groups to the parents in their school districts. There are some university classes in parent education.

Churches are interested in Adlerian parent study groups, as many see the principles consistent with their religious beliefs. Adlerian societies throughout the world offer parent study groups. Community organizations and parent groups, as well as mental health agencies and professionals in private practice, have hosted or made referrals to parent study groups.

A parent study group leader does not have to be an expert in Adlerian principles of parent-child relationships. The Adlerian material the group is studying serves as the authority for the group. The leader's job is basically to facilitate discussion and involvement. Therefore, lay persons can lead parent study groups. Consequently, more groups can be conducted in a community by using lay leaders instead of just relying on busy professionals. If professionals do initially establish groups, we suggest they look for parents in their

Oscar C. Christensen, Ed.D.

groups who would be effective group facilitators. The professional, with group experience, can train these potential group leaders in leadership skills and then act in a supervisory and support role. Also, the professional can run follow-up experiences for parent study group graduates (See following sections).

Topics

The topics chosen by leaders largely depends upon the Adlerian program they are using. Obviously, the more Adlerian principles one teaches, the better understanding parents will have of the concepts. At the very minimum, the following basic four concepts should be taught.

1. Understanding behavior and misbehavior

2. Encouragement

3. Natural and logical consequences

4. The family meeting

In our opinion, to give parents a broader experience, information on emotions and communication skills can be extremely helpful. Parents need to understand how children use emotions to manipulate adults and how the parents' own emotions can reinforce children's mistaken goals. Learning how to listen and help children discuss problems that face them in their lives, builds a positive relationship and teaches problem-solving skills. When parents learn how to express their feelings about children's misbehavior in non-threatening ways, children often respect the parents' feelings and are more cooperative. The children also learn appropriate ways to express their feelings about things others do which they find upsetting. Expressing and hearing each other's feelings paves the way for negotiation on disagreements. Communication skills are also a tremendous aid in conducting effective family meetings.

Session Formats

The most effective session formats appear to be those which include a variety of activities. The variety of activities keeps parents interested and provides for different learning styles. An effective format could include:

- Discussion of participants' experiences in applying principles taught in a previous session.

- A discussion of a reading assignment.

- Media, either visual, audio or both.
- An exercise on the concepts.
- A summary of the session.
- Assignments (both behavioral and reading) for the next session.

With the exception of some exercises, the group needs to be seated in a circle so that everyone can see everyone else. This arrangement facilitates discussion. We suggest the participants not be seated behind labels as this creates a psychological barrier between people.

It is important to encourage continued interaction between participants. This interaction keeps the session moving and maintains interest.

Some groups like to serve refreshments and take a break in mid-session. Others serve refreshments which are readily available and no break is taken. If refreshments are served, it's important to rotate the responsibility among the participants for the refreshments. In this way, participants experience the democratic nature of the philosophy—shared responsibility.

Time Limits and Size

Time is always a limitation in presenting any topic. Most Adlerian parent study groups run for 8 to 10 weeks for 1 1/2 to 2 hours per weekly session, depending upon how the program is organized.

Since group involvement is essential in parent study groups, they need to be kept small enough to provide opportunity for maximum interaction. We find 10 to 12 members to be an ideal size for a parent study group.

Getting Organized

There is a great interest in parent education today, so the participants are out there; the problem is how to reach them. School counselors and other educational professionals can present the idea of a parent study group at a PTA or PTO meeting. During the meeting, the potential leader can give the rationale for parent study groups, an overview of the Adlerian philosophy, answer questions and distribute a sign-up sheet. Also, flyers can be sent home with the students indicating what the experience will involve, perhaps a list of topics, and/or typical problems which will be discussed such as bedtime, fighting among siblings, homework, etc. Time and place of the meetings are listed, and you may want a preregistration form.

Churches can send out similar notices and announce the groups during services. Agencies and those in private practice may want to form groups from individual family counseling clients, or distribute posters in churches, schools and public places where parents are likely to see them. Sometimes newspapers and radio and television will give space for public service announcements.

Whether you present the concept at a public gathering of parents, or in a flyer, it's important to point out that joining a parent study group does not indicate deficiency but rather an interest in improving parent-child relationships. Also indicate that these groups are intended for typical parents with typical parent-child concerns, not for those with children with serious problems who may need private counseling. Again, these are educational groups, not therapy groups.

Once you get your group together, you'll want to get acquainted. A useful getting acquainted procedure, which also helps cohese the group, is to have all in turn give their names and the names and ages of their children in descending order, oldest to youngest. This information can then be put on a piece of oak-tag, folded in half so they stand up and so that everyone in the group can see the participants' names and the names and ages of their children. These signs are good for reference. Collect the cards after each meeting as they have a way of disappearing if the participants take them home! Here's an example of what we mean:

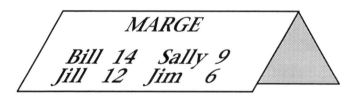

Next, ask parents, one at a time, to briefly name one challenge with their children they would like to solve as a result of being in the group. List each challenge on a large piece of primary or "butcher" paper with the person's name beside it. This can then be displayed in each group meeting. The leader can refer to the list when a person's problem has been dealt with. The leader can ask, "We dealt with your concern this session, did you get some ideas?" Cross off the person's name and concern as they are dealt with.

As the parents mention the names and ages of their concerns, point out any similarities among parents on these items. In this way, parents begin to learn their concerns are shared by others. (See Leadership Skills.)

Next, distribute materials and take care of any other housekeeping items, such as refreshments, possible changes in schedule, etc. Then you want to get a commitment from each parent in your group to attend all of the sessions. You might say, "This program runs for 10 weeks. Is everyone willing to attend each session?" Some may be skeptical because they don't know what it's all about. But, do encourage them to attend at least three or four sessions to get a better understanding of the principles. Then, if some just won't "buy" the philosophy, they may wish to drop out.

Next, outline the objectives of the program, or what they will learn, "Our objective is to study these materials to see how they will help us establish more effective relationships with our children. Some of the things we will be learning are how to understand our children's misbehavior, how to encourage them and ways to help children develop self-discipline."

Establish and explain some ground rules or discussion guidelines. Have them written down and display them each week where all can see them. Examples:

1. Stay on the topic.
2. Become involved in the discussion.
3. Share the time.
4. Be patient—take one step at a time.
5. Encourage each other.
6. Be responsible for your own behavior (Dinkmeyer & McKay, 1989, Leader's Manual, p. 46-47).

As you go through the ground rules, explain that these have been helpful in guiding other discussion groups. Ask for comments and any additional suggestions for rules. Get a commitment to the guidelines.

The guidelines are very useful for group self-discipline. If a member of the group gets off task, the leader can ask, "What guideline are we forgetting?"

Leader Qualifications and Characteristics

Even beginning leaders can be effective if they follow a preestablished program, such as the ones we will mention. The main qualifications for leaders are that they have a genuine interest in people and parenting and have some ability to facilitate discussion groups. As we said earlier, both professionals and lay persons can lead parent study groups .

The role of a parent study group leader is that of a facilitator, not an expert. The program you're using becomes the expert. The leader's job is to organize the group, present the program, facilitate discussions and exercises, get the people involved with the materials and each other, provide encouragement, make homework assignments and help the participants apply the concepts.

Effective leaders realize that parents learn more by interacting with each other than they do from looking to the leader for all the answers. When leaders function as facilitators rather than experts, they utilize the resources of the group and model the democratic philosophy they are trying to teach.

Even if you are an expert on parent-child relationships, you will be more effective if you avoid playing that role. For one thing, you can't possibly live up to everyone's expectations of an expert. So, if you play that role, you may set yourself up for defeat. The parents may lose confidence in you.

Certainly, anyone who is going to lead a parent study group needs to be familiar with the philosophy that's being presented. So do your homework, but let the program be the authority.

You don't have to defend anything in the program you're using. If a person disagrees, ask your group to comment.

Since you are an equal member of the group, you do have a right to give your opinion. But make sure the group knows it's your opinion and not the "Gospel." Some helpful statements for phrasing your opinions are: "In my opinion," "I see it this way," or "I think the authors mean."

We suggest you give your opinion last and only if it's necessary. If you give your opinion when it's not needed, the group may tend to put you in the role of the expert.

Explain your role at the first meeting and clarify any misconceptions of your role or the program. You could say, "We're here to study this philosophy and see how it may apply to your families. The program will be our authority. All of you will have to make you own decision on whether or not to accept the program's suggestions."

Please realize that people may try to place you in the role of the expert even though you don't want to play that role. To avoid this, redirect questions and comments made to you about the program to the group: "What do others think about this?"

Effective leaders believe in the capacity of people to improve their situations. They are optimistic and positive, seeing people's potential. They are always ready to utilize the group to provide encouragement. Effective leaders believe in mutual respect and equality. They believe that each person is responsible for one's own behavior. They recognize that while one can't change another's behavior, people can change their own behavior and influence others. Effective leaders allow people to accept the consequences of their decisions.

Leadership Skills

An effective leader possesses certain skills to help the group run smoothly and productively. These skills are essential for facilitating a parent study group in a democratic fashion. We will discuss 10 skills (Dinkmeyer & McKay, 1989). The skills are not difficult to learn, nor are all skills used in the same session. The skills employed depend upon what's needed at any given point in a session.

1. **Structuring** refers to the purpose of the group, limits of the discussion, topics, time, and so forth. From the very beginning the leader needs to state the purpose of the group and clear up any misconceptions. Explain that the group is designed to be a course in child rearing and not group therapy. They will be discussing ideas presented by the authors of the program to see how they apply to their own situations. Individual concerns will be discussed only as they relate to the topic at hand. If members spend most of their time discussing their concerns, little time will be left to learn the principles and skills which will help them learn how to deal with their problems. Leaders need to fully explain what the group will be doing, the limitation on discussing individual concerns, and the rationale. If this is not clearly explained and accepted by members, the group will degenerate into a "coffee klatch" type of experience with little learning.

Oscar C. Christensen, Ed.D.

Introducing the group's ground rules is also part of the initial structuring process. Make sure the parents understand and accept the guidelines.

At times during the meetings you will need to structure. The group may be spending more time on an issue, for instance, than is productive. Respectfully tell them "We've discussed this for _____ , and we have a lot to cover. Could we move on and come back to this later if there's time?"

While structuring may, at first, sound autocratic, it is not meant to be. The skill is used strictly to keep the group within certain guidelines to make the experience productive. Groups tend to get off track without an identified and accepted specific structure.

2. **Universalizing** involves identifying common concerns of members. Most parents come to the group with a certain amount of anxiety. Some think "I'd better be quiet, or the others will think I'm a bad parent." When the leaders show how they feel, then the others feel it's okay to bring up issues and answer questions. The skill is especially important in early meetings and can begin as parents are getting acquainted and sharing concerns they would like to get answers to as the group proceeds. After each person states a concern, simply ask "Does anyone else have this concern?"

As the group proceeds, you can universalize whenever it seems needed: "Has any one else had difficulty putting this principle into practice"

3. **Linking** refers to identifying common and unique elements of member's comments. As members comment, the leader listens for links between member's comments. This skill aids in the universalizing process. For example, Susan may be talking about problems with bed wetting. The leader may remember that George was talking about the same problem with his child in an earlier session. The leader could say, "Sounds like you and George have something in common. It seems both of you have this experience."

Sometimes members will comment on problems which, on the surface, seem different, when they are really the same. For example, Maria may be talking about how difficult it is to get her son Carlos to eat. Earlier Joan was discussing her difficulty in getting Kristin to do chores. While these problems seem different, the goal of the child in each instance may be power. You can point this out to the parents. "While Maria is talking about her difficulty in getting Carlos to eat, this seems similar to what Joan shared with us about trying to get Kristin to do chores. Both kids seem be using the goal of power. Do you see the similarity?" These kinds of links help members learn the principles. In this case, look for the goal in the interaction.

At other times problems may appear similar, when they are actually different, that is, the children in each incident are displaying the same behavior, but their goals are different. For example, both Bill and Mike are talking about bedtime problems with their children. You note that Bill's son Jack is using bedtime problems to gain attention, while Mike's daughter Jenny, is after power. The problems are not really the same. Each child will need a different parental response to avoid reinforcing the goal and to redirect the child's misbehavior. You could say, "While both Bill and Mike have problems getting their kids to bed, the children seem to have different goals. Jack seems to want attention while Jenny is displaying her power." Again, linking in this fashion helps the group learn the principles.

As your group begins to learn more, you can ask them to link. You could say, "Do you see any similarity (or differences) between these problems?"

4. **Giving Feedback** is a skill that helps members learn how they are perceived by the group. There are two kinds of feedback: reflective and confrontive.

Reflective feedback refers to communicating that you understand how a member feels. When a parent expresses a concern, you can use reflective listening to help the parent feel understood: "Sounds like you're pretty discouraged." You can also ask the group to provide reflective feedback: "How do you think Jim is feeling?"

Confrontive feedback involves showing a member how one's behavior may be affecting the group. This feedback also gives parents insight into how they might be perceived by children. Confrontive feedback is to learn how they may be perceived. The person receiving the feedback must make the decision about changing one's behavior.

The feedback must be presented in a respectful, caring way. Example: "When you talk in an angry tone, I feel like I'm being attacked. I wonder if your children may feel the same way?" The leader can also ask for feedback from the group. "How did you feel when Juan said that?"

Confrontive feedback is often uncomfortable for the senders as well as the receivers, but when a person's behavior is adversely affecting the group and possibly one's children, it's essential to give the person the information. Certainly there needs to be cohesion in the group and an atmosphere of caring before this skill is used.

You promote confrontive feedback by modeling and talking about its purpose: "When we respectfully tell people how they are coming across, we help them gain understanding on how their behavior may be affecting their children. We show people we care when we risk commenting on their behavior. Yet they have to decide whether or not to change their behavior."

5. **Identifying the child's goal** involves making guesses about the child's goal of misbehavior in a parent-child interaction reported by a member. This is a skill the parents must learn if they are to effectively identify the child's goal and plan an appropriate alternative.

   There are four questions the leader needs to ask to help the group identify the child's goal when a member brings up a concern.

   • What specifically did the child do?
   • How did you feel?
   • What did you do and what happened?
   • (To the group) Based on these clues, what do you think is the child's goal?

6. **Providing Encouragement** refers to focusing on members and their children's strengths, resources, efforts, improvements, and contributions. Encouragement instills faith in parents and children. It is the most important skill in leading parent study groups. Encouragement makes the difference between success and failure of a group.

   The leader needs to look for opportunities to provide encouragement for members and to get them to encourage each other and their children. The leader, for instance, can note improvement: "You may feel you have not reached your goal, but look at the progress you've made. Last week you _____ and this week you _____." It's also important to call for encouragement from the group. "Who notices the improvement Jan has made from what she told us last week and what's happening now?" When a member is discussing a problem with a difficult child, the leader can say, "Yes, there certainly are a lot of problems, but what are Carla's strengths that you can build on?"

7. **Setting Tasks and Obtaining Commitments** refers to putting the program's skills into action. While it's interesting to sit around and discuss Adlerian ideas, nothing much will come of it unless the parents are willing to experiment with the skills in their own families.

Most Adlerian programs have activity homework assignments that parents are expected to do between meetings. For example, when encouragement is discussed, the parents are asked to practice encouragement that week. Effective programs give parents a chance to discuss their experience the next week.

At times during a session, a need for other commitments will arise. For example, you may be discussing problems that are appropriate for logical consequences. A parent indicates a problem similar to the one being discussed. As the leader, you can ask the parent if one is willing to experiment with a logical consequence for the problem during the week. First, ask the parent specifically what one is willing to do and under what conditions. If the parent needs help, ask the group for suggestions. For example, a mother may want to get out of fights between her children. She decides that each time they fight, she will take herself out of the situation and go to the bathroom. She will remain there until the fight is over (unless it appears dangerous, of course).

Watch out for the "I'll try" trap. When most people say they will try to do something it usually means one of two things. Either they don't believe it will work and are trying to "buy some insurance," or they really want to do it but want to get you off their back. They can then clear their conscience by saying, "Well, at least I tried," or "I knew it wouldn't work anyway—I showed you!" So, when someone says "I'll try," respectfully challenge their intentions: "When I hear someone say 'I'll try' it seems to me they're either not sure or convinced it won't work." Since things take time to change, would you be willing to experiment with the new skill for a week? Regardless of what happens (except for danger) you'll keep doing it and then we'll talk about it to see how things went?" If the person is not willing, that's okay. Often, though, you can get them to make a commitment to simply think about the idea. If they give you this commitment, they'll often not only think about it, they'll actually do it!

Oscar C. Christensen, Ed.D.

8. **Summarizing** is the process of pulling the discussion together at any appropriate point in the meeting. While final summaries are important, they are not the only summaries that may be needed. For example, after a long discussion, before moving on, you may want to summarize or ask the group to do so. After there's been disagreement, you can summarize or ask the group to do so. After there's been disagreement, you can summarize or call for one. "It seems we're not in agreement on this. Some feel _____ and others feel _____ ." Could we move on and come back to this later if there's time and interest?"

The final summary involves getting the group's impression of what they've learned. This helps clear up any misconceptions because sometimes what's taught is not what's learned. Each person can complete the statement "I learned." You can also ask the group for any suggestions for improving the sessions that are within the guidelines of the program.

9. **Redirecting** is the process of maximizing group involvement. When the leader gets a direct statement of questions from the group, the leader redirects the comment by "fielding" it to the group, "What do you think about that?" "How do others feel?" "What would the authors say about that?" If an inappropriate suggestion is made concerning what a member might do about a problem shared, the leader can redirect by asking, "What might happen if that is done?"

Sometimes redirecting involves brainstorming. When parents are giving suggestions to a member on what she or he can do about a problem, creativity is stifled if the receiving member beings to reject suggestions. But, if the member is encouraged to suspend evaluation until all ideas are given, the other members feel free to generate possibilities. Then, after the brainstorming is concluded, the receiving member is asked which idea is most appealing.

10. **Promoting Direct Interaction** is a method for getting members to talk to each other instead of directing their comments through the leader. When a member comments about another member, such as, what can be done about a challenge with one's child, the leader promotes direct interaction by asking the commenting member to speak directly to the other parent: "Would you tell _____?"

Maintaining Group Direction

When groups begin, most members are looking forward to the experience, even though they may be somewhat anxious. Many have unrealistic expectations of the leader and the program. They expect all their problems with their children will be solved. You need to make your role clear and let them know that the program will offer many ideas to help them, but they will need to take the responsibility for implementing the ideas.

In this initial stage of the group, many will want instant answers to their concerns. Remind them that change takes time, while acknowledging the validity of their questions. The program cannot be taught all at once and they need to be willing to take things one step at a time. For example, one needs to understand the four goals of misbehavior to be in a position to understand a child's goal, before one can develop appropriate options.

As the group moves along, some members may lose enthusiasm for the program, especially when they are experiencing difficulty in changing their behavior. Many parents expect their child to change while they continue to behave the same way. When they finally realize that changes in their children occur only when they change, they may begin to doubt the value of the program. If this happens, be prepared to restate the purpose of the program and give a lot of encouragement by recognizing effort and improvement. Utilize the more confident members of the group to help the disgruntled members maintain their interest. You can also use procedures to stimulate interest like exercises and role playing.

Once you get through this discouragement, your group has usually regained their commitment. They are assuming responsibility for their own behavior. They are cohesive and interested in helping each other.

Oscar C. Christensen, Ed.D.

Dealing with Resistance in Parent Study Groups

As a group leader you will find that some parents will take to these ideas readily and others will resist. Resistance is defined as existing when a group member is at cross purposes with the leader, other members, the program or all three. The task is to attempt to achieve a mutual purpose through motivational procedures.

Group members may resist for a variety of reasons: (1) they don't really understand the concepts, (2) their experience is very different, (3) they are not sure the ideas will work, or (4) they are playing a "game" that is, resistance is their characteristic way of dealing with any idea—not just parenting information—which is different from their own view of the world.

Some members resist through challenging the leader and/or program. Involve the group, unless you think the person will feel attacked. The group can help you motivate the challenger. Redirect by asking, "What do others think?" "What's happening in our group?" "What do you think _____ is really saying?" "What guideline are we forgetting?"

If group involvement is ineffective, first reflect the member's feelings, e.g., "You seem uncomfortable with this principle." Then, ask the member to make a value judgment about one's methods or beliefs in terms of the consequences the children: "Are you satisfied with your relationship with your children?" Or, "Is what you're doing working for you?"

If the person concludes that the relationship is not satisfying, or the methods aren't working, ask, "Are you willing to experiment with these principles and delay your judgment for a few weeks?" Get a commitment to using the principles for a specific period of time.

If the person judges methods and beliefs as satisfying or effective, ask the member to consider the consequences of the procedures by saying something like, "You mean once you punish your children for something they never do it again?" If the person admits the methods don't have lasting results, ask if that person would like the children to be more cooperative and if one is willing to experiment and suspend judgment.

If the person is still resisting, you could ask, "What do you want for your children when they grow up and leave home?" Most reply that they want the children to be responsible, happy, etc. Then ask, "Do you think your present methods will help you achieve these goals?" If the member then realizes your point, ask the member if one is willing to experiment.

Let's consider what you could do if your reluctant member is still resisting. You can use the "Godfather Principle" (You know, make him an offer he can't refuse!) in a humorous way. For example, you could say, "Are you saying that if you continue to drag Johnny out of bed, force him to eat everything that's put before him, to do his homework, etc., one day he'll just automatically take on these responsibilities without someone, such as his wife, to prod him into it?" Or, you could say, "It seems to me you are providing personal maid service, cleaning his room, and so forth. How long do you want to do this?" Another way, "Do you expect John might get married some day? Do you plan to move in with him, or train his wife to take your place?" Or, as Oscar Christensen would say: "Pampered children may be fun when they're young but would you want your son to marry one?"

For those who insist on being involved in their children's school work, and have higher education goals for their children, one can say, "Do you want John to go to college some day?" "Do you plan to go with him ?"

If this does not stop the resistance, they may be into a "game" and it's time to remind them of the purpose of the program by structuring. "You will have to make your own decision as to whether these ideas will work for you. It's not for us to try to force you. We need to move on now."

Some people resist by playing the role of the authority—citing personal experience as expert testimony, or quoting other authorities in childrearing who represent a different approach. First, redirect to the group: "What's happening in our group?" or "What guideline are we forgetting?" If this does not bring results, reflect with something like, "You find these other ideas appealing." And, finally, if the person still wants to debate philosophies, structure by stating the purpose of the program. "We are here to learn how to apply the ideas in this program, not to debate other approaches. We need to move on." Clarify your role as the leader in helping members learn what the program has to offer.

A member may resist by stating that "kids will be kids" and give excuses for children's misbehavior, accepting children's misbehavior as normal and can't be changed or just a stage they are going through. Again, redirect to the group, "What do others think?" If this is not effective, structure: "You apparently think that relationships can't be improved, but others have found that they can improve their relationships. We are studying these methods because we believe we can change relationships. We hope you will find this out too." Then move on to something else.

You may encounter a member who proclaims that one's spouse, the child's teacher, grandparents, and so forth are the cause of all the child's problems and that these people must change before anything will improve. This person is disclaiming any responsibility for changing. Redirect to the group: "What do you think _____ is really saying?" If group comments are ineffective, carry the person's proclamation to the extreme: "You seem to be saying that nothing you do has any effect on your relationship with Sharon." If the member is still resistant, clarify the purpose of the program: "We are here to learn what we can do, not what others should do. The only behavior we can change is our own. I think if you will concentrate on what you can do to make things better, you will see positive results, but you have to decide what you want to do." Then move on.

The catastrophizer can present difficulties for the leader. This is the member who proclaims "What do you do when, or what if?" to ideas in the program or other member's suggestions. Such a person can be dealt with effectively by first determining if the expressed problem will be dealt with in a later session; if so, inform the person when it will be covered and move on. If it will not be covered later, ask the person: "Have you ever experienced the problem you are worried about?" If the person has experienced such a problem, ask for a specific example and determine the goal and specific procedures for dealing with the issue. If the member has not experienced the expressed concern but fears it may happen, redirect to the group: "What would you do?" "What principle would apply in this situation?" If the member continues it's quite possible that person is playing a "game," The person does not want to change but wants to demonstrate good intentions by proving that the ideas just won't work because "horrible" things will "happen!" At this point, it's appropriate to say: "It seems to me that when you continue to say 'what if,' you are trying to find reasons for not changing." If this is not effective, you could say, "I guess anything could happen, but let's consider our actual experiences." Then proceed with the other members or the next section.

The "yes but-er" often appears in a group. This is the person who really does not want to change but does want to create a good impression. This person agrees with everything that is said and then cancels the agreement by saying "but," or synonyms such as except, although, however, still, and so on. In effect the person first agrees with the idea, then there's the "but" followed by reasons why the idea won't work. First, redirect the group: "What do you think ____ is really saying?" If this doesn't work, confront the person with: "When I hear you say 'yes, but,' I get the feeling that you are discussing an idea that you really don't want to use and that's okay, it's not our purpose to try to force you." Move on.

One who monopolizes a group can ruin it if not handled effectively. With the monopolizer it is suggested that you don't involve the group as the person may feel attacked. Direct the attention away from the member: "Let's hear what others have to say." Tell the person that you need to move on and if there's time you'll return to those concerns. If none of these procedures work, you will need to talk with the person individually. Sometimes giving the monopolizer an assignment is effective. "I'm having trouble getting all the group members involved in the discussion. Would you help me by making a tally of the number of times each member talks next session?" Or, get the person to take notes by proclaiming a "bad" memory. If these suggestions don't help, you may want to confront the member with an I message: "When we keep discussing your comments, I feel frustrated because I can't get the other members involved with the program and each other." Finally, you may have to ask the member to drop the group and seek individual family counseling where more time can be devoted to those concerns.

When you encounter behavior similar to what's been described here, don't automatically assume the member is going to be a problem. Wait and see what happens. That person may simply want more information and initial resistance may be the way of obtaining it. It won't take you very long to determine who your most challenging parents will be.

Also, please note that any of the above suggested procedures for dealing with difficult members must be used with mutual respect.

Oscar C. Christensen, Ed.D.

Programs for Parent Study Groups

The following popular programs are suggested for Adlerian parent study groups. We will describe each program here and give complete references at the end of this chapter.

Children: The Challenge

Dr. Dreikurs and Vickie Soltz's book, *Children: The Challenge* (1964) is often referred to as the "Bible" of Adlerian parent study groups. The book has been translated into several languages including German, Spanish, and Hebrew. The topics in *Children: The Challenge* include autocratic to democratic shifts in society, equality and mutual respect, life style formation, the four goals of misbehavior, encouragement, replacing reward and punishment with natural and logical consequences and the family council.

Many of the chapters are very brief. Dreikurs and Soltz devoted a chapter to each of their 34 child rearing principles rather than group them in fewer, longer chapters. *Children: The Challenge* is available in both hardback and paperback.

In 1967 Vickie Soltz wrote *Study Group Leader's Manual*, which is designed for leaders using *Children: The Challenge* (1964). The study guide included: Reasons for Study Groups, Benefits of Group Study, Goal of a Parent Study Group, Techniques of Leadership, Character of the Group, Traits of an Effective Leader, Coping with the Problem Members and Problems from the Group, How to Prepare for the First Meeting, Time Limits, and Group Size. The book also contained study outlines, questions and supplementary reading. The method of group study basically involves reading materials between sessions and discussing them during the sessions. An occasional tape and/or filmstrip is recommended. Parents are expected to practice the skills between sessions. The outline suggested 10 sessions where the chapters are grouped into topic areas.

Raising a Responsible Child

This book, *Raising a Responsible Child,* by Dinkmeyer and McKay (1973), has also gained popularity in study group circles. The book has been translated into German, Japanese, and Greek.

Raising a Responsible Child (1973) expanded on Dreikurs' work and blended communication skills with the basic principles of Adler and Dreikurs. The book also contained a series of self-checks for parents to determine the child's goal of misbehavior and to identify the reasons for any problems encountered in using the book's concepts.

While there is currently no published study guide for *Raising a Responsible Child,* many leaders have developed their own guides. The book does have a suggested study outline in the final chapter.

Raising a Responsible Child is also available in both hardback and paperback.

The STEP Programs

The STEP (Systematic Training for Effective Parenting) Programs are multimedia materials. *Early Childhood STEP* (1989), *STEP/Teen* (1983, 1990) and *The Next STEP (1987)* all grew out of *STEP* (1976, 1989). Each program integrates communication skills and rational emotive therapy with Adlerian principles.

STEP is a nine-session program primarily for parents of children age six to preteen. *Early Childhood STEP* is a seven-session program for parents of children under six. This program integrates developmental psychology and Adlerian psychology. *STEP/Teen* is a ten-session program for parents of preteens through adolescence. *The Next STEP* is a six-session advanced program for graduates of a basic parent study group.

The programs include the following components:

- **Leaders' guides.** Among the leader's guide contents are information on how to generate parent study groups, how to organize group sessions, leadership skills and how to deal with difficult group members. Each sessions has a detailed, step-by-step lesson guide including discussion questions and skill building exercises.

- **Video or audio cassettes.** Each cassette contains vignettes of parent-child interactions which stop at the point of parental response. The group discusses each incident, and gives their opinion of a solution. Then the tape is resumed so parents can compare their conclusions with those of the authors.

- **Discussion gudelines posters.** These guidelines provide the ground rules for effective group discussion. They are discussed in the first session and displayed throughout the program for reference.

- **Parents' books.** Each program includes a parent book which contains brief chapters pertaining to session topics. The books are illustrated with cartoons. Additional parts of the handbook include:

1. **Points to Remember.** These are summary statements of the basic concepts of each lessons. There is one Points to Remember page for each session.

2. **Charts.** The charts summarize a major concept from each sessions. They are used for discussion in the group sessions.

3. **Exercises.** The exercises help participants understand and apply the concepts to their own families. Some involve parent-child issues and some focus on personal growth of the parent.

4. **Publicity Aids.** Announcement posters, invitational fliers, camera-ready ad slicks, public service announcements, and news releases are included to help leaders generate groups.

- **Supplementary materials.** The following materials are also available:

  1. **STEP for Substance Abuse Prevention.** This booklet infuses substance abuse prevention information into the *STEP* or *STEP/Teen* programs and shows how *STEP* skills aid in parents' prevention efforts.

  2. **STEP Audio Handbook.** Two cassettes contain the content of the Parent's Handbook—the parent book for *STEP.*

New Beginnings:
Skills for Single Parents and Stepfamily Parents

New Beginnings (Dinkmeyer & McKay, 1987) is a *STEP*-style program for single and stepfamily parents. This eight-session program applies the *STEP*-skills to these populations and provides additional information to parents for coping with non-nuclear family situations.

Summary

In this chapter we have discussed parent study groups, what they are, why they are needed, and how to set them up. Topics for parent study groups and session formats were outlined, as well as qualifications and skills for effective leaders, how to maintain group direction, programs for parent study groups, and leadership training. We wish you good luck in your efforts to educate parents in Adlerian principles.

References

Dinkmeyer, D., & McKay, G.D. (1973). *Raising a responsible child: Practical steps to successful family relationships.* New York: Simon & Schuster.

Dinkmeyer, D., & McKay, G.D. (1981). *Padres eficaces con entrenamiento sistematico (PECES).* Spanish language edition of *STEP).* Circle Pines, MN: American Guidance Service.

Dinkmeyer, D., & McKay, G.D. (1989). *Systematic training for effective parenting (STEP).* (rev. ed.). Circle Pines, MN: American Guidance Service.

Dinkmeyer, D., & McKay, G.D. (1990). *STEP/Teen* (rev. ed.). Circle Pines, MN: American Guidance Service.

Dinkmeyer, D., & McKay, G.D., & Dinkmeyer, J.S. (1989). *Early childhood STEP.* Circle Pines, MN: American Guidance Service.

Dinkmeyer, D., & McKay, G.D., & Dinkmeyer, J.S. (1991). *Early childhood STEP* (Spanish language edition). Circle Pines, MN: American Guidance Service.

Dinkmeyer, D., & McKay, G.D., Dinkmeyer, D. Jr., Dinkmeyer, J.S., & McKay, J.L. (1987). *The next STEP: Effective parenting through problem solving.* Circle Pines, MN: American Guidance Service.

Dinkmeyer, D., & McKay, G.D., & McKay, J.L. (1987). *New beginnings: Skills for single and stepfamily parents.* Champaign, IL: Research Press.

Dreikurs, R., & Soltz, V. (1964). *Children: The challenge.* New York: Hawthorn.

Stoltz, V. (1967). *Study group leader's manual.* Chicago: Adler School of Professional Psychology.